I0465426

SAFEGUARDING
NATIONS

Cybersecurity Strategies for African Government Departments...

Temitope Olodo Esq.,

Contents

DEDICATION

This book is dedicated to my beloved wife, NG, for her love and determination to partner with me to achieve greatness.

ACKNOWLEDGEMENT

I acknowledge the contribution of my children, Abisha and Zuriel to my work on cybersecurity.

I appreciate my colleagues in the CT community and members of the Africa Security Forum (worldwide) who always strive to improve safety and security in Africa through constructive dialogue.

ABSTRACT

In an increasingly digital world, the protection of government departments in Africa against cyber threats is paramount to national security and governance.

This abstract delves into the imperative of cybersecurity strategies tailored for African government departments. It highlights the challenges faced by governments in the region, such as limited resources and evolving threat landscapes, and underscores the importance of building resilient cyber defences.

African governments can enhance their cyber resilience and safeguard national assets through collaboration, capacity building, and adherence to regulatory frameworks.

This abstract provides insights into the key components of effective cybersecurity strategies for African government departments. It emphasizes the urgent need for concerted action to address cyber threats in the region.

@ 2024 – **Safeguarding Nations: Cybersecurity Strategies for African Government Departments**

This publication is designed to provide accurate and authoritative information regarding the subject matter covered.

It is sold with the understanding that the publisher is not engaged in rendering legal or other professional services. If legal advice or other expert assistance is required, the services of a competent professional should be sought.

Copyright © 2024

All rights reserved

Printed in the United States of America

ISBN................................

No part of this book may be used or reproduced in any manner whatsoever without written permission except in the case of brief quotations embodied in critical articles and reviews.

For more information about the author, conference speaking engagement and purchase of bulk copies of this book visit - www.traz.org

Twitter - @temitopeolodo

Facebook - temitopeolodo

First Edition

Chapter 1: Introduction

The Imperative of Cybersecurity for Government Departments in Africa

In an era defined by digital transformation and interconnectedness, the imperative of cybersecurity for government departments in Africa cannot be overstated. As nations across the continent embrace technology to drive socio-economic development and improve governance, they also face escalating cyber threats that endanger national security, undermine public trust, and jeopardize critical infrastructure. This book explores the pressing need for robust cybersecurity measures within African government departments, examines the unique challenges they encounter, and outlines strategies to mitigate cyber risks effectively.

Cyber Threat Landscape in Africa:

Africa's digital landscape is characterized by rapid digitization, increasing internet penetration, and widespread adoption of mobile technology. While these advancements offer immense opportunities for growth and innovation, they also expose governments to a myriad of cyber threats. From nation-state actors seeking to infiltrate government networks for espionage or sabotage to cybercriminal organizations engaging in ransomware attacks and data breaches, the spectrum of cyber threats facing African governments is diverse and evolving. Moreover, the proliferation of digital platforms and online services has expanded the attack surface, making government departments vulnerable to phishing scams, malware infections, and social engineering tactics.

Challenges Facing African Government Departments: African government departments confront a multitude of challenges in effectively addressing cybersecurity threats. Limited financial resources and budget constraints often hamper efforts to invest in cybersecurity infrastructure, technologies, and skilled personnel. Moreover, the shortage of cybersecurity professionals exacerbates the vulnerability of government networks and systems. Additionally, the lack of comprehensive regulatory frameworks and enforcement mechanisms leaves government departments without clear guidelines for cybersecurity compliance and risk management. Furthermore, the rapid pace of technological innovation and the prevalence of legacy systems within government agencies present significant obstacles to implementing robust cybersecurity measures.

The Impact of Cyber Attacks on National Security and Governance:

Cyber-attacks targeting government departments in Africa can have far-reaching consequences, compromising national security, undermining public trust, and disrupting essential services. Breaches of sensitive government data can result in the theft of classified information, intellectual property, and personally identifiable information, posing significant risks to national security and sovereignty. Moreover, cyber-attacks on critical infrastructure, such as energy grids, transportation systems, and healthcare facilities, can disrupt vital services, endanger public safety, and impede socio-economic development. Additionally, the erosion of public trust in government institutions due to cybersecurity incidents can have political ramifications, leading to diminished confidence in governance and electoral processes.

Strategies for Enhancing Cybersecurity in African Government Departments:

To effectively address the cybersecurity challenges facing African government departments, comprehensive strategies must be implemented. Firstly, governments must prioritize cybersecurity as a national priority and allocate sufficient resources to build cyber resilience. This includes investing in cybersecurity infrastructure, technologies, and workforce development initiatives. Additionally, governments should establish robust regulatory frameworks that mandate cybersecurity standards and require government departments to adhere to best practices for risk management and compliance. Moreover, fostering collaboration and information sharing among government agencies, industry stakeholders, and international partners is essential for enhancing situational awareness and responding effectively to cyber threats. Furthermore, governments should prioritize cybersecurity awareness and education initiatives to empower government employees with the knowledge and skills necessary to recognize and mitigate cyber risks.

In conclusion, the imperative of cybersecurity for government departments in Africa cannot be overstated. As the continent continues to embrace digital transformation and leverage technology to drive development, the need to safeguard government networks, systems, and data against cyber threats becomes increasingly critical. By investing in cybersecurity infrastructure, implementing robust regulatory frameworks, fostering collaboration, and promoting cybersecurity awareness and education, African governments can enhance their cyber resilience and protect national interests in an ever-evolving threat landscape.

Overview of Cyber Threats Facing African Governments

As African governments increasingly digitize their operations and services, they become more susceptible to a wide range of cyber threats. These threats, which include cyber-attacks, data breaches, and other malicious activities, pose significant challenges to national security, economic stability, and public trust. This book provides an overview of the cyber threats facing African governments, explores their impact on governance and society, and outlines strategies to address and mitigate these threats effectively.

1. The Landscape of Cyber Threats in Africa:

- Africa's digital transformation has created new opportunities for innovation and growth but has also attracted the attention of cybercriminals, state-sponsored actors, and hacktivist groups.

- Cyber threats facing African governments encompass a diverse array of tactics, including malware attacks, phishing scams, ransomware incidents, and distributed denial-of-service (DDoS) attacks.

- These threats target government networks, critical infrastructure, financial systems, and sensitive data, posing risks to national security, economic stability, and public safety.

2. Malware Attacks:

- Malware, including viruses, worms, trojans, and ransomware, poses a significant threat to African governments by exploiting vulnerabilities in software and systems.

- Malware attacks can result in the theft of sensitive information, financial losses, and disruption of government services.

- African governments must deploy robust antivirus software, implement regular software updates and patches, and educate employees about the dangers of malware to mitigate these threats effectively.

3. Phishing Scams:

    - Phishing scams involve the use of deceptive emails, websites, or messages to trick individuals into revealing sensitive information, such as passwords, usernames, or financial details.

    - Phishing attacks targeting government employees can lead to unauthorized access to government networks, data breaches, and identity theft.

    - African governments should implement email filtering systems, conduct regular phishing awareness training for employees, and encourage the use of multi-factor authentication to thwart phishing attempts.

4. Ransomware Incidents:

    - Ransomware attacks involve the encryption of files or systems by cybercriminals, who demand payment (usually in cryptocurrency) for the decryption key.

- Ransomware incidents can disrupt government operations, cause financial losses, and compromise sensitive data.

- African governments must implement robust backup and recovery mechanisms, maintain up-to-date cybersecurity software, and establish incident response plans to mitigate the impact of ransomware attacks.

5. Distributed Denial-of-Service (DDoS) Attacks:

- DDoS attacks involve flooding government websites or networks with a high volume of traffic, causing them to become unavailable to legitimate users.

- DDoS attacks can disrupt government services, undermine public trust, and impact economic activities.

- African governments should collaborate with internet service providers (ISPs) to implement DDoS mitigation strategies, such as traffic filtering and rate limiting, to mitigate the impact of DDoS attacks.

6. Insider Threats:

- Insider threats involve individuals within government organizations who misuse their access privileges to steal sensitive information, sabotage systems, or facilitate cyber-attacks.

- Insider threats can be particularly challenging to detect and mitigate due to the trusted status of the individuals involved.

- African governments should implement robust access controls, monitor user activity, and conduct regular security awareness training to mitigate the risk of insider threats.

7. Impact on Governance and Society:

- Cyber threats facing African governments have far-reaching implications for governance, society, and economic development.

- These threats can undermine public trust in government institutions, compromise national security, and impede socio-economic progress.

- Addressing cyber threats requires a multi-faceted approach that involves collaboration between government agencies, private sector stakeholders, and international partners.

In conclusion, the cyber threats facing African governments are diverse, sophisticated, and evolving. From malware attacks and phishing scams to ransomware incidents and insider threats, these threats pose significant challenges to national security, economic stability, and public trust. African governments must prioritize cybersecurity efforts, implement robust defence mechanisms, and foster collaboration to address and mitigate these threats effectively. By investing in cybersecurity infrastructure, raising awareness, and building partnerships, African governments can enhance their cyber resilience and safeguard national interests in an increasingly digital world.

Importance of Developing Comprehensive Cybersecurity Strategies

In an era defined by digital interconnectedness and rapid technological advancement, the importance of developing comprehensive cybersecurity strategies cannot be overstated. As organizations and individuals increasingly rely on digital platforms and technologies to conduct business, communicate, and access information, they become more susceptible to cyber threats.

From data breaches and ransomware attacks to phishing scams and insider threats, the cyber landscape is fraught with risks that can have far-reaching consequences. This book explores the critical importance of developing comprehensive cybersecurity strategies and outlines key components of an effective approach to cyber defence.

1. Understanding Cybersecurity:

    - Cybersecurity refers to the practice of protecting computer systems, networks, and data from unauthorized access, cyber-attacks, and other malicious activities.

    - The goal of cybersecurity is to safeguard sensitive information, maintain the integrity of systems, and ensure the availability of critical services.

    - Cybersecurity encompasses a wide range of technologies, processes, and practices designed to prevent, detect, and respond to cyber threats effectively.

2. Evolving Threat Landscape:

- The threat landscape in cyberspace is constantly evolving, with cybercriminals employing increasingly sophisticated tactics and techniques to exploit vulnerabilities and infiltrate systems.

- Cyber threats can originate from a variety of sources, including nation-state actors, criminal organizations, hacktivist groups, and insider threats.

- Common cyber threats include malware attacks, phishing scams, ransomware incidents, and distributed denial-of-service (DDoS) attacks.

3. Risks to Organizations and Individuals:

- Cyber threats pose significant risks to organizations and individuals, ranging from financial losses and reputational damage to legal liabilities and regulatory penalties.

- Data breaches can result in the theft of sensitive information, such as personal data, financial records, and intellectual property, leading to identity theft, fraud, and privacy violations.

- Ransomware attacks can cripple business operations, disrupt critical services, and extort victims for financial gain, causing significant economic harm and reputational damage.

4. Importance of Comprehensive Cybersecurity Strategies:

- Developing comprehensive cybersecurity strategies is essential for organizations and individuals to effectively mitigate cyber risks and safeguard their assets.

- A comprehensive cybersecurity strategy encompasses a range of components, including risk assessment, threat intelligence, incident response, and employee training.

- By taking a proactive and holistic approach to cybersecurity, organizations can identify and mitigate vulnerabilities, detect and respond to threats in a timely manner, and recover from cyber incidents with minimal disruption.

5. Key Components of Cybersecurity Strategies:

- Risk Assessment: Conducting regular risk assessments to identify and prioritize cybersecurity risks based on their likelihood and potential impact.

- Threat Intelligence: Gathering and analysing threat intelligence to understand the tactics, techniques, and procedures employed by cyber adversaries and anticipate emerging threats.

- Security Controls: Implementing a layered approach to security, including access controls, encryption, firewalls, intrusion detection systems, and endpoint security solutions.

- Incident Response: Establishing incident response plans and procedures to effectively respond to cyber incidents, including containment, eradication, recovery, and post-incident analysis.

- Employee Training: Providing comprehensive cybersecurity awareness and training programs to educate employees about cyber risks, best practices, and their role in defending against cyber threats.

6. Collaboration and Information Sharing:

- Collaboration and information sharing are critical components of effective cybersecurity strategies, enabling organizations to leverage collective intelligence, resources, and expertise to detect and respond to cyber threats more effectively.

- Collaboration can take various forms, including partnerships with industry peers, government agencies, law enforcement, and cybersecurity organizations.

- Information sharing platforms and initiatives facilitate the exchange of threat intelligence, best practices, and lessons learned, enabling organizations to stay ahead of evolving cyber threats.

7. Continuous Improvement and Adaptation:

- Cybersecurity is an ongoing process that requires continuous improvement, adaptation, and evolution to address emerging threats, vulnerabilities, and technologies.

- Organizations must regularly review and update their cybersecurity strategies, policies, and controls to reflect changes in the threat landscape and their business environment.

- By embracing a culture of continuous improvement and learning, organizations can enhance their cyber resilience and effectively defend against evolving cyber threats.

In conclusion, the importance of developing comprehensive cybersecurity strategies cannot be overstated in today's digital world. Cyber threats pose significant risks to organizations and individuals, ranging from financial losses and reputational damage to legal liabilities and regulatory penalties. By developing comprehensive cybersecurity strategies that encompass risk assessment, threat intelligence, security controls, incident response, employee training, collaboration, and continuous improvement, organizations can effectively mitigate cyber risks and safeguard their assets. Investing in cybersecurity is not only a prudent business decision but also a critical imperative for ensuring the security, integrity, and resilience of digital ecosystems.

Chapter 2: Understanding Cybersecurity

Introduction to Understanding Cybersecurity

In an increasingly digitized world where technology permeates every aspect of our lives, cybersecurity stands as the frontline defence against a multitude of threats that lurk in the digital realm. As we navigate the complexities of cyberspace, understanding cybersecurity becomes paramount for individuals, organizations, and governments alike. This introductory statement serves as a gateway to delve into the multifaceted landscape of cybersecurity, exploring its significance, principles, and implications.

1. Significance of Cybersecurity:

- Cybersecurity plays a pivotal role in safeguarding sensitive information, critical infrastructure, and personal privacy from malicious actors seeking to exploit vulnerabilities in digital systems.

- In today's interconnected world, where data is the lifeblood of modern economies and societies, the protection of digital assets is essential for maintaining trust, integrity, and stability.

- Cybersecurity encompasses a broad spectrum of disciplines, ranging from technology and policy to human behaviour and ethics, highlighting its interdisciplinary nature and far-reaching impact.

2. Principles of Cybersecurity:

- At its core, cybersecurity is guided by a set of fundamental principles that underpin effective defence strategies. These principles include confidentiality, integrity, availability, authentication, and non-repudiation.

- Confidentiality ensures that sensitive information is only accessible to authorised individuals or entities, safeguarding it from unauthorised disclosure or access.

- Integrity ensures the accuracy and reliability of data by protecting it from unauthorized modification, deletion, or tampering.

- Availability ensures that digital assets and services are accessible and usable when needed, preventing disruptions or downtime that could impact operations.

- Authentication verifies the identity of users and devices, ensuring that only authorized individuals or entities are granted access to digital resources.

- Non-repudiation ensures that actions or transactions cannot be denied or falsely attributed, providing accountability and traceability in digital interactions.

3. Implications of Cybersecurity:

- The implications of cybersecurity extend beyond the realm of technology to encompass economic, social, and geopolitical dimensions.

- In the business world, cybersecurity breaches can result in financial losses, reputational damage, and legal liabilities, impacting the bottom line and eroding stakeholder trust.

- In the public sector, cybersecurity incidents can compromise national security, disrupt critical infrastructure, and undermine public trust in government institutions.

- On a societal level, cybersecurity threats can exacerbate inequalities, exacerbate digital divides, and erode individual privacy and civil liberties, raising ethical and moral concerns.

4. Importance of Cybersecurity Awareness:

- Building cybersecurity awareness is essential for empowering individuals and organizations to recognize, mitigate, and respond to cyber threats effectively.

- Cybersecurity awareness encompasses education, training, and outreach efforts aimed at promoting best practices, raising threat awareness, and fostering a culture of cyber hygiene.

- By enhancing cybersecurity awareness, individuals can become more vigilant against phishing scams, malware attacks, and other cyber threats, reducing the likelihood of successful cyber attacks.

Understanding cybersecurity is paramount in today's digital age, where the proliferation of technology brings unprecedented opportunities and risks. By grasping the significance, principles, and implications of cybersecurity, individuals, organizations, and governments can better navigate the complexities of cyberspace and safeguard their digital assets and interests. As we embark on this journey of understanding cybersecurity, let us embrace the collective responsibility to promote a secure and resilient digital ecosystem for generations to come.

Fundamentals of Cybersecurity: Concepts and Terminology

In an increasingly interconnected and digitalized world, cybersecurity has emerged as a critical discipline for protecting sensitive information, critical infrastructure, and personal privacy from a myriad of cyber threats. Understanding the fundamentals of cybersecurity, including its key concepts and terminology, is essential for individuals, organizations, and governments to effectively navigate the complex landscape of cyber defence. This book provides an in-depth exploration of the fundamentals of cybersecurity, offering insights into its core concepts, principles, and terminology.

1. Definition and Scope of Cybersecurity:

   - Cybersecurity, also known as information security or IT security, encompasses the practice of protecting computer systems, networks, and data from unauthorized access, cyber-attacks, and other malicious activities.

   - The scope of cybersecurity extends beyond technology to include policies, processes, and practices aimed at safeguarding digital assets, ensuring data confidentiality, integrity, and availability, and mitigating cyber risks effectively.

2. Key Concepts of Cybersecurity:

   - Confidentiality: Ensuring that sensitive information is only accessible to authorized individuals or entities and protected from unauthorized disclosure or access.

   - Integrity: Maintaining the accuracy, reliability, and trustworthiness of data by protecting it from unauthorized modification, deletion, or tampering.

- Availability: Ensuring that digital assets, services, and resources are accessible and usable when needed, preventing disruptions or downtime that could impact operations.

- Authentication: Verifying the identity of users and devices to ensure that only authorized individuals or entities are granted access to digital resources.

- Authorization: Granting permissions and privileges to users based on their authenticated identity and predefined access rights, limiting their access to specific resources and functionalities.

- Non-repudiation: Ensuring that actions or transactions cannot be denied or falsely attributed, providing accountability and traceability in digital interactions.

3. Common Cyber Threats and Attack Vectors:

- Malware: Malicious software designed to disrupt, damage, or gain unauthorized access to computer systems, including viruses, worms, trojans, spyware, and ransomware.

- Phishing: Social engineering tactic used to trick individuals into revealing sensitive information, such as passwords, usernames, or financial details, through deceptive emails, websites, or messages.

- Denial-of-Service (DoS) and Distributed Denial-of-Service (DDoS) Attacks: Overloading computer systems, networks, or services with a high volume of traffic to disrupt or disable them, rendering them unavailable to legitimate users.

- Insider Threats: Malicious or negligent actions by individuals within an organization, such as employees, contractors, or business partners, who misuse their access privileges to steal sensitive information, sabotage systems, or facilitate cyber-attacks.

- Advanced Persistent Threats (APTs): Sophisticated and stealthy cyber-attacks orchestrated by skilled adversaries, such as nation-state actors or organized crime groups, aimed at compromising targeted organizations for espionage, sabotage, or financial gain.

4. Cybersecurity Terminology:

- Vulnerability: Weakness or flaw in a system, application, or network that could be exploited by cyber attackers to compromise its security.

- Exploit: Technique or tool used to take advantage of a vulnerability in a system, application, or network to gain unauthorized access, execute malicious code, or achieve other nefarious objectives.

- Patch: Software update or fix released by vendors to address known vulnerabilities and security weaknesses in their products, applications, or systems.

- Firewall: Network security device or software that monitors and controls incoming and outgoing network traffic based on predetermined security rules, policies, or access controls.

- Encryption: Process of converting plaintext data into ciphertext using cryptographic algorithms and keys to protect it from unauthorized access or interception during transmission or storage.

- Intrusion Detection System (IDS) and Intrusion Prevention System (IPS): Security solutions that monitor network traffic, detect suspicious or malicious activities, and alert or block potential threats in real-time.

5. Principles of Cybersecurity:

• Defence-in-Depth: Layered approach to security that employs multiple defensive measures, such as firewalls, antivirus software, intrusion detection systems, and access controls, to protect against cyber threats.

• Least Privilege: Principle of providing users with the minimum level of access privileges and permissions necessary to perform their job functions, reducing the risk of unauthorized access or misuse of resources.

• Patch Management: Process of regularly applying software updates, patches, and security fixes to address known vulnerabilities and security weaknesses in software, applications, and systems.

• Incident Response: Coordinated process of detecting, responding to, and recovering from cybersecurity incidents, such as data breaches, malware infections, or network intrusions, to minimize their impact and restore normal operations.

In conclusion, understanding the fundamentals of cybersecurity, including its key concepts and terminology, is essential for individuals, organizations, and governments to effectively protect against cyber threats. By grasping the core principles, concepts, and terminology of cybersecurity, stakeholders can better navigate the complex landscape of cyber defence, mitigate risks, and safeguard digital assets and interests. As the cyber threat landscape continues to evolve and grow in complexity, ongoing education, training, and awareness are critical to staying abreast of emerging threats and emerging technologies. Through collective efforts and a proactive approach to cybersecurity, we can build a more secure and resilient digital future for all.

Types of Cyber Threats Targeting Government Departments

Government departments around the world face a multitude of cyber threats that pose significant risks to national security, public safety, and critical infrastructure. These threats, ranging from sophisticated cyber-attacks orchestrated by nation-state actors to opportunistic cybercriminal activities, underscore the importance of robust cybersecurity measures within government agencies. This book provides an in-depth analysis of the types of cyber threats targeting government departments, exploring their characteristics, motivations, and implications.

1. Advanced Persistent Threats (APTs):

• APTs are sophisticated and stealthy cyber-attacks orchestrated by skilled adversaries, such as nation-state actors, intelligence agencies, or organized crime groups, with the aim of compromising targeted government agencies for espionage, sabotage, or financial gain.

• APTs typically involve a combination of advanced techniques, including social engineering, spear phishing, and zero-day exploits, to infiltrate government networks, exfiltrate sensitive information, and maintain persistent access for extended periods without detection.

• APT actors often employ advanced malware, such as custom-designed remote access trojans (RATs) or advanced persistent malware (APM), to evade detection by traditional security measures and maintain covert control over compromised systems.

2. Insider Threats:

• Insider threats involve malicious or negligent actions by individuals within government agencies, such as employees, contractors, or trusted partners, who misuse their access privileges to steal sensitive information, sabotage systems, or facilitate cyber-attacks.

• Insider threats can take various forms, including unauthorized data exfiltration, data manipulation, or sabotage of critical infrastructure, and can have significant consequences for national security, public safety, and government operations.

• Insider threat actors may be motivated by various factors, including financial gain, ideological beliefs, or personal grievances, and may exploit vulnerabilities in organizational processes, policies, or controls to carry out their malicious activities.

3. Nation-State Cyber Attacks:

• Nation-state cyber-attacks are orchestrated by governments or state-sponsored hacking groups with the aim of infiltrating government networks, stealing sensitive information, disrupting critical infrastructure, or conducting cyber espionage for geopolitical or strategic purposes.

• Nation-state actors often possess advanced capabilities and resources, including sophisticated cyber weapons, zero-day exploits, and extensive intelligence-gathering capabilities, enabling them to launch highly targeted and coordinated cyber operations against government targets.

• Nation-state cyber-attacks can have significant geopolitical implications, leading to diplomatic tensions, economic sanctions, and retaliatory measures between nations, and can undermine trust and cooperation in cyberspace.

4. Ransomware Incidents:

• Ransomware attacks involve the deployment of malicious software (ransomware) by cybercriminals to encrypt data on government systems and demand payment (usually in cryptocurrency) in exchange for the decryption key.

• Ransomware incidents can disrupt government operations, compromise sensitive information, and result in financial losses and reputational damage for affected agencies.

• Ransomware actors often target government departments with the expectation of receiving significant ransom payments due to the critical nature of government data and the potential impact of data loss or system downtime.

5.   Phishing and Social Engineering:

• Phishing and social engineering tactics involve the use of deceptive emails, messages, or websites to trick government employees into revealing sensitive information, such as passwords, usernames, or financial details, or to download malicious software onto government systems.

• Phishing attacks targeting government departments often impersonate trusted entities, such as government agencies, colleagues, or business partners, to lure victims into clicking on malicious links, opening infected attachments, or disclosing confidential information.

• Phishing and social engineering attacks can lead to unauthorized access to government networks, data breaches, and compromise of sensitive information, posing significant risks to national security and public trust.

6.   Supply Chain Attacks:

• Supply chain attacks involve targeting third-party vendors, contractors, or suppliers that have access to government networks or systems as a means of infiltrating government departments and compromising their security.

• Supply chain attacks can take various forms, including the insertion of malicious code or backdoors into software or hardware components, the compromise of software update mechanisms, or the manipulation of supply chain logistics to deliver counterfeit or compromised products.

• Supply chain attacks pose significant challenges for government departments, as they may exploit trust relationships and dependencies within the supply chain ecosystem to bypass traditional security controls and gain unauthorized access to government networks.

In conclusion, government departments face a wide range of cyber threats that pose significant risks to national security, public safety, and critical infrastructure. From sophisticated APTs orchestrated by nation-state actors to opportunistic ransomware attacks conducted by cybercriminals, the threat landscape facing government agencies is diverse and constantly evolving.

By understanding the characteristics, motivations, and implications of these cyber threats, government departments can better prepare and defend against cyber-attacks, implement robust cybersecurity measures, and safeguard national interests in an increasingly digital world. Collaboration, information sharing, and investment in cybersecurity capabilities are essential for enhancing the resilience and security of government networks and systems against emerging cyber threats.

Impact of Cyber Attacks on National Security and Governance

In an interconnected and digitized world, the impact of cyber-attacks on national security and governance cannot be overstated. From nation-state cyber espionage campaigns targeting critical infrastructure to cybercriminal activities aimed at disrupting government operations, cyber-attacks pose significant threats to the integrity, stability, and sovereignty of nations. This book delves into the multifaceted impact of cyber-attacks on national security and governance, exploring their implications for governments, economies, societies, and international relations.

1. Disruption of Critical Infrastructure:

• Cyber-attacks targeting critical infrastructure, such as energy grids, transportation systems, and healthcare facilities, can have catastrophic consequences for national security and public safety.

• Disruption or compromise of critical infrastructure can lead to widespread power outages, transportation disruptions, healthcare emergencies, and loss of life, causing significant economic damage and social upheaval.

• Nation-state adversaries may target critical infrastructure as part of cyber warfare campaigns to weaken the resilience and capacity of their adversaries, undermine public confidence in government institutions, and achieve strategic objectives.

2. Theft of Sensitive Information:

• Cyber-attacks aimed at stealing sensitive information, such as classified government documents, intellectual property, and personally identifiable information (PII), pose grave threats to national security, economic competitiveness, and individual privacy.

• Nation-state actors may engage in cyber espionage campaigns to gain access to sensitive government information, military secrets, and diplomatic communications, providing them with strategic advantages in geopolitical conflicts and negotiations.

• The theft of intellectual property through cyber-attacks can undermine innovation, research, and development efforts, depriving nations of economic opportunities and technological advancements.

3. Compromise of Government Networks and Systems:

• Cyber-attacks targeting government networks and systems can compromise the integrity, confidentiality, and availability of critical government services and operations.

• Breaches of government networks can result in unauthorized access to sensitive information, manipulation of government data, and disruption of government operations, leading to erosion of public trust, loss of confidence in government institutions, and political instability.

- Government agencies responsible for national defence, law enforcement, and intelligence may be particularly vulnerable to cyber-attacks, as they store and manage highly classified and sensitive information essential for safeguarding national security and public safety.

4. Economic Impact:

- Cyber-attacks can have significant economic repercussions for nations, including financial losses, decreased investor confidence, and disruption of business operations.

- The costs associated with mitigating cyber-attacks, restoring affected systems, and implementing cybersecurity measures can impose substantial financial burdens on governments, businesses, and taxpayers.

• Cyber-attacks targeting critical infrastructure, financial institutions, and supply chains can disrupt economic activities, disrupt supply chains, and undermine consumer confidence, leading to reduced productivity, job losses, and economic downturns.

5. Social and Political Consequences:

• Cyber-attacks can have profound social and political consequences, including erosion of public trust in government institutions, polarization of public opinion, and escalation of geopolitical tensions.

• Public awareness of cyber threats and vulnerabilities can shape perceptions of government competence, transparency, and accountability, influencing electoral outcomes, policy decisions, and public discourse.

• The attribution of cyber-attacks to nation-state actors or foreign adversaries can trigger diplomatic crises, economic sanctions, and retaliatory measures between nations, exacerbating international tensions and instability.

6.   Legal and Regulatory Implications:

•   Cyber-attacks may have legal and regulatory implications for governments, including obligations to investigate and prosecute cyber criminals, strengthen cybersecurity regulations, and enhance data protection laws.

•   Governments may face pressure to enhance international cooperation and information sharing to combat cyber threats effectively, promote cybersecurity capacity building, and establish norms of responsible behaviour in cyberspace.

•   The development of cyber defence strategies, incident response plans, and cybersecurity frameworks becomes imperative for governments to mitigate cyber risks, protect national interests, and uphold the rule of law in cyberspace.

In conclusion, the impact of cyber-attacks on national security and governance is far-reaching and multifaceted, encompassing economic, social, political, and legal dimensions. From disrupting critical infrastructure and compromising sensitive information to undermining public trust in government institutions and escalating geopolitical tensions, cyber-attacks pose significant threats to the integrity, stability, and sovereignty of nations. Addressing these challenges requires concerted efforts by governments, businesses, civil society, and international partners to enhance cybersecurity resilience, promote responsible behaviour in cyberspace, and uphold the principles of security, stability, and prosperity in the digital age.

By investing in cybersecurity capabilities, fostering collaboration, and strengthening regulatory frameworks, nations can better defend against cyber threats, protect national interests, and ensure a secure and resilient digital future for all.

Chapter 3: Cybersecurity Landscape in Africa

In recent years, the African continent has experienced rapid technological advancements and widespread digitization, transforming societies, economies, and governance structures. As Africa embraces the opportunities presented by the digital age, it also grapples with the challenges posed by cyber threats and vulnerabilities. Chapter 3 of our book delves into the cybersecurity landscape in Africa, offering insights into the unique dynamics, trends, and challenges shaping cybersecurity efforts across the continent.

1. Emergence of Cybersecurity as a Priority:

• With the proliferation of digital technologies and internet connectivity, cybersecurity has emerged as a critical priority for African nations seeking to protect their digital infrastructure, secure sensitive data, and safeguard national interests.

• Governments, businesses, and civil society organizations in Africa are increasingly recognizing the importance of investing in cybersecurity capabilities, raising awareness about cyber threats, and fostering collaboration to enhance cyber resilience and mitigate risks effectively.

2.   Overview of Cyber Threats:

• Africa faces a diverse range of cyber threats, including malware attacks, phishing scams, ransomware incidents, and distributed denial-of-service (DDoS) attacks, which target government agencies, businesses, critical infrastructure, and individuals.

• The threat landscape in Africa is characterized by both opportunistic cybercriminal activities and sophisticated cyber espionage campaigns orchestrated by nation-state actors, posing significant challenges for cybersecurity efforts across the continent.

3.   Unique Dynamics and Challenges:

•   The cybersecurity landscape in Africa is shaped by unique dynamics and challenges, including limited cybersecurity awareness and education, inadequate cybersecurity infrastructure and resources, and a lack of comprehensive regulatory frameworks and enforcement mechanisms.

•   Many African countries face constraints in terms of financial resources, technical expertise, and institutional capacity to address cybersecurity challenges effectively, hindering their ability to defend against cyber threats and mitigate risks.

4.   Regional Initiatives and Collaboration:

•   Despite these challenges, African nations are increasingly embracing regional initiatives and collaboration to enhance cybersecurity resilience, promote information sharing, and build cybersecurity capacity across the continent.

- Regional organizations, such as the African Union (AU), the Economic Community of West African States (ECOWAS), and the Southern African Development Community (SADC), play a pivotal role in coordinating cybersecurity efforts, fostering collaboration among member states, and developing regional cybersecurity frameworks and strategies.

5.   Case Studies and Best Practices:

- Chapter 3 features case studies and best practices highlighting successful cybersecurity initiatives, innovative approaches, and lessons learned from across the African continent.

- These case studies showcase examples of effective public-private partnerships, capacity-building programs, and cybersecurity awareness campaigns that have contributed to strengthening cybersecurity resilience and promoting a culture of cyber hygiene in Africa.

6.   Future Outlook and Recommendations:

•   The chapter concludes with a discussion of the future outlook for cybersecurity in Africa and recommendations for policymakers, government agencies, businesses, and civil society organizations to enhance cybersecurity capabilities, address emerging cyber threats, and promote a secure and resilient digital ecosystem across the continent.

•   Key recommendations include investing in cybersecurity infrastructure and capacity building, strengthening regulatory frameworks, promoting cybersecurity awareness and education, and fostering regional collaboration and information sharing.

In summary, Chapter 3 provides a comprehensive overview of the cybersecurity landscape in Africa, examining the unique dynamics, challenges, initiatives, and best practices shaping cybersecurity efforts across the continent. By understanding the evolving cybersecurity landscape in Africa and embracing collaborative approaches, stakeholders can work together to address cyber threats effectively, build cyber resilience, and promote a secure and prosperous digital future for Africa.

Current State of Cybersecurity Infrastructure in African Governments

In recent years, African governments have made significant strides in digitizing their operations and embracing technology to drive economic growth, improve service delivery, and enhance governance. However, with increased connectivity and digitalization comes the heightened risk of cyber threats and attacks. This book explores the current state of cybersecurity infrastructure in African governments, examining the challenges, opportunities, and initiatives aimed at strengthening cyber resilience across the continent.

1. Overview of Cybersecurity Infrastructure:

•   Cybersecurity infrastructure refers to the systems, technologies, policies, and practices put in place by governments to protect their digital assets, networks, and data from cyber threats.

• In African governments, cybersecurity infrastructure encompasses a range of components, including firewalls, intrusion detection systems (IDS), antivirus software, encryption tools, incident response plans, and cybersecurity awareness programs.

2. Challenges Facing Cybersecurity Infrastructure in African Governments:

• Limited Financial Resources: Many African governments face budget constraints and competing priorities, making it challenging to allocate sufficient resources to cybersecurity initiatives and infrastructure.

• Lack of Technical Expertise: There is a shortage of skilled cybersecurity professionals in Africa, with a limited pool of experts trained in cybersecurity best practices, incident response, and threat analysis.

• Inadequate Regulatory Frameworks: Some African countries lack comprehensive cybersecurity laws, regulations, and standards, leading to gaps in cybersecurity governance and enforcement mechanisms.

• Insufficient Cybersecurity Awareness: Low levels of cybersecurity awareness among government employees and citizens contribute to susceptibility to social engineering attacks, phishing scams, and other cyber threats.

• Legacy Systems and Infrastructure: Many African governments rely on outdated and legacy IT systems and infrastructure, which may lack built-in security features and be more vulnerable to cyber-attacks.

3. Initiatives to Strengthen Cybersecurity Infrastructure:

• Capacity Building and Training: African governments are investing in capacity-building programs and training initiatives to develop a skilled workforce capable of addressing cybersecurity challenges effectively.

•   Public-Private Partnerships: Collaboration between government agencies, private sector stakeholders, and international organizations is essential for sharing expertise, resources, and best practices in cybersecurity.

•   Adoption of Cybersecurity Frameworks: Some African countries are adopting cybersecurity frameworks, such as the National Institute of Standards and Technology (NIST) Cybersecurity Framework, to guide the development and implementation of cybersecurity policies and practices.

•   Establishment of Computer Emergency Response Teams (CERTs): CERTs play a crucial role in coordinating incident response, sharing threat intelligence, and facilitating collaboration among government agencies and other stakeholders in responding to cyber threats.

•   Awareness and Education Campaigns: Governments are launching cybersecurity awareness campaigns and educational initiatives to raise awareness about cyber threats, promote good cyber hygiene practices, and empower citizens to protect themselves online.

4. Case Studies: Examples of Cybersecurity Infrastructure in African Governments:

• Kenya:

The Kenyan government has established the National Kenya Computer Incident Response Team Coordination Centre (National KE-CIRT/CC) to enhance cybersecurity coordination, incident response, and information sharing among government agencies, private sector entities, and other stakeholders.

• Nigeria:

The Nigerian government has launched the National Cybersecurity Policy and Strategy (NCPS) to provide a framework for addressing cyber threats, protecting critical infrastructure, and promoting a secure digital ecosystem in Nigeria.

• South Africa:

The South African government has developed the National Cybersecurity Policy Framework (NCPF) to guide the implementation of cybersecurity initiatives, strengthen cybersecurity governance, and enhance collaboration across government departments and sectors.

5. Future Outlook:

• Despite the challenges, there are reasons for optimism regarding the future of cybersecurity infrastructure in African governments.

• With increased awareness of cyber threats, growing investments in cybersecurity, and enhanced collaboration among stakeholders, African governments are better positioned to strengthen their cybersecurity posture and mitigate cyber risks effectively.

• However, sustained commitment, continued investments, and ongoing collaboration will be essential to address the evolving cyber threat landscape and build a resilient cybersecurity infrastructure that can protect African governments and citizens in the digital age.

In conclusion, the current state of cybersecurity infrastructure in African governments is characterized by both challenges and opportunities. While resource constraints, technical skills shortages, and regulatory gaps pose significant obstacles, initiatives such as capacity building, public-private partnerships, and cybersecurity frameworks are helping to strengthen cyber resilience across the continent.

By investing in cybersecurity infrastructure, fostering collaboration, and raising awareness about cyber threats, African governments can better protect their digital assets, secure critical infrastructure, and promote a safe and secure digital environment for all citizens.

Challenges and Constraints Faced by African Governments in Ensuring Cyber Resilience

In an increasingly digitalized world, African governments face numerous challenges and constraints in ensuring cyber resilience. The rapid growth of technology adoption and digital connectivity across the continent has led to increased cyber threats and vulnerabilities, placing immense pressure on governments to protect critical infrastructure, secure sensitive data, and safeguard national interests. This book explores the multifaceted challenges and constraints faced by African governments in building cyber resilience and mitigating cyber risks effectively.

1. Limited Financial Resources:

• One of the primary challenges facing African governments in ensuring cyber resilience is the limited availability of financial resources. Many countries on the continent struggle with budget constraints and competing priorities, making it challenging to allocate sufficient funds to cybersecurity initiatives and infrastructure.

• Limited financial resources hinder governments' ability to invest in cybersecurity technologies, tools, and expertise, as well as to implement comprehensive cybersecurity awareness and education programs.

2. Lack of Technical Expertise:

• The shortage of skilled cybersecurity professionals is a significant constraint for African governments. There is a scarcity of individuals trained in cybersecurity best practices, incident response, threat analysis, and cybersecurity governance.

• The lack of technical expertise hampers governments' ability to develop and implement effective cybersecurity strategies, respond to cyber incidents promptly, and stay abreast of evolving cyber threats and trends.

3. Inadequate Regulatory Frameworks:

• Many African countries lack comprehensive cybersecurity laws, regulations, and standards, leading to gaps in cybersecurity governance and enforcement mechanisms. The absence of robust regulatory frameworks makes it challenging for governments to address cyber threats effectively and hold perpetrators accountable.

- Inadequate regulatory frameworks also contribute to inconsistencies in cybersecurity practices and standards across different sectors and industries, hindering efforts to build a cohesive and coordinated cyber resilience strategy.

4. Insufficient Cybersecurity Awareness:

- Low levels of cybersecurity awareness among government officials, employees, and citizens pose a significant challenge for African governments. Many individuals lack basic knowledge about cyber threats, best practices for protecting themselves online, and the potential consequences of cyber-attacks.

- Insufficient cybersecurity awareness increases the likelihood of falling victim to social engineering attacks, phishing scams, and other cyber threats, compromising government networks, data, and systems.

5. Legacy Systems and Infrastructure:

- African governments often rely on outdated and legacy IT systems and infrastructure, which may lack built-in security features and be more vulnerable to cyber-attacks. Legacy systems are often difficult and costly to update, maintain, and secure, making them attractive targets for cybercriminals.

• The reliance on legacy systems hinders governments' ability to implement modern cybersecurity technologies and practices, such as encryption, multi-factor authentication, and threat intelligence, to protect against emerging cyber threats.

6. International Cooperation and Collaboration:

• Limited international cooperation and collaboration pose challenges for African governments in addressing transnational cyber threats and cybercrime. Many cyber-attacks originate from foreign actors or are orchestrated across national borders, requiring coordinated efforts and information sharing among countries.

• African governments may face obstacles in collaborating with international partners, sharing threat intelligence, and extraditing cyber criminals due to legal, jurisdictional, and diplomatic challenges.

7.   Socio-economic Factors:

•   Socio-economic factors, such as poverty, inequality, and lack of access to education and employment opportunities, can exacerbate cybersecurity challenges in Africa. Individuals facing economic hardship may resort to cybercrime as a means of livelihood, contributing to the proliferation of cyber threats and attacks.

•   Addressing underlying socio-economic factors is essential for building a resilient cyber ecosystem and reducing the incentives for engaging in cybercriminal activities.

Conclusion:
In conclusion, African governments face numerous challenges and constraints in ensuring cyber resilience, ranging from limited financial resources and technical expertise to inadequate regulatory frameworks and cybersecurity awareness. Addressing these challenges requires a multifaceted approach that encompasses investments in cybersecurity infrastructure, capacity building, regulatory reform, public awareness

campaigns, and international cooperation. By addressing the underlying root causes of cybersecurity challenges and adopting a holistic and collaborative approach, African governments can enhance cyber resilience, protect critical infrastructure, and safeguard national interests in an increasingly digitalized world.

Case Studies Highlighting Cyber Incidents in African Countries

Cyber incidents are a growing concern for governments across the African continent, as digitalization and connectivity increase vulnerability to cyber threats. From targeted attacks on critical infrastructure to widespread data breaches affecting government agencies, cyber incidents have significant implications for national security, public trust, and economic stability.

This book presents case studies highlighting notable cyber incidents in African countries, exploring their causes, impacts, and implications for cybersecurity resilience.

1. Kenya: 2019 National Hospital Ransomware Attack

• In 2019, Kenya's national hospital network experienced a ransomware attack that paralyzed critical healthcare services across the country. The attack targeted the hospital's IT systems, encrypting patient records, medical data, and administrative files, rendering them inaccessible.

• The ransomware attack disrupted patient care, forced hospitals to revert to manual record-keeping processes, and delayed medical procedures and appointments. The government declared a state of emergency and launched a coordinated response to restore services and mitigate the impact of the attack.

• The incident highlighted the vulnerabilities of critical infrastructure to cyber-attacks and underscored the need for robust cybersecurity measures and contingency plans to protect essential services and ensure continuity of operations.

2. Nigeria: 2020 Central Bank Cyber Heist

- In 2020, Nigeria's central bank fell victim to a cyber heist orchestrated by a sophisticated cybercriminal syndicate. The attackers exploited vulnerabilities in the bank's internal network and payment systems to transfer millions of dollars to offshore accounts.

- The cyber heist caused significant financial losses for the central bank, disrupted banking operations, and eroded public confidence in the country's financial system. The government launched an investigation into the incident and implemented measures to strengthen cybersecurity defences and prevent future attacks.

- The incident highlighted the challenges of defending against advanced cyber threats and the importance of implementing robust cybersecurity controls, monitoring systems, and incident response protocols to detect and mitigate cyber-attacks promptly.

3. South Africa: 2017 Government Data Breach

• In 2017, South Africa's government suffered a major data breach that exposed the personal information of millions of citizens, including names, addresses, ID numbers, and financial records. The breach occurred due to a vulnerability in a government database that was exploited by cybercriminals.

• The data breach raised concerns about the security of government databases, the protection of citizens' privacy rights, and the adequacy of cybersecurity measures within government agencies. The government faced criticism for its slow response to the breach and lack of transparency in communicating with affected individuals.

• The incident underscored the importance of securing sensitive data, implementing robust access controls and encryption mechanisms, and enhancing cybersecurity awareness and training for government employees.

4. Ghana: 2018 Electoral Commission Website Hack

•   In 2018, Ghana's Electoral Commission website was hacked by a group of cyber activists who defaced the site and posted political messages criticizing the government and electoral process. The hack occurred during a period of heightened political tension in the country.

•   The website defacement drew attention to vulnerabilities in the electoral commission's web infrastructure and raised concerns about the security of election systems and processes. The incident prompted the government to enhance cybersecurity measures and monitor online threats during electoral periods.

•   The hack highlighted the potential for cyber-attacks to disrupt democratic processes, undermine public trust in institutions, and influence political outcomes, emphasizing the need for robust cybersecurity defences to protect against cyber threats to electoral integrity.

Conclusion:

These case studies illustrate the diverse range of cyber incidents affecting African countries and their significant implications for national security, public trust, and economic stability. From ransomware attacks on critical infrastructure to data breaches exposing sensitive information, cyber incidents underscore the importance of prioritizing cybersecurity resilience and investing in robust defence measures.

By learning from these incidents, African governments can enhance their cybersecurity posture, strengthen defences against cyber threats, and mitigate risks to safeguard national interests and citizen welfare in an increasingly digitalized world.

Chapter 4: Building Resilient Government Cyber Defences

As cyber threats continue to evolve in complexity and sophistication, governments around the world face growing challenges in defending their digital infrastructure, protecting sensitive data, and safeguarding national security interests. Chapter 4 of our book focuses on the imperative of building resilient government cyber defences in the face of escalating cyber threats and vulnerabilities. This introduction provides an overview of the chapter's key themes, objectives, and contributions to understanding and enhancing government cybersecurity resilience.

1.   Evolution of Cyber Threat Landscape:

•   The chapter begins by examining the evolving cyber threat landscape, highlighting the proliferation of cyber-attacks targeting government agencies, critical infrastructure, and national interests. From nation-state cyber espionage campaigns to ransomware attacks and insider threats, governments confront a diverse range of cyber threats that pose significant risks to their operations and security.

2.   Importance of Cyber Resilience:

•   Building on the understanding of the cyber threat landscape, the chapter emphasizes the importance of cyber resilience for government agencies. Cyber resilience encompasses the ability to anticipate, withstand, recover from, and adapt to cyber-attacks, ensuring the continuity of government operations, the protection of critical assets, and the preservation of national security interests.

3.   Key Components of Resilient Cyber Defences:

•   The chapter explores the key components of resilient cyber defences for government agencies, including comprehensive cybersecurity strategies, robust technical controls, effective incident response capabilities, and a culture of cybersecurity awareness and accountability. These components are essential for mitigating cyber risks, detecting and responding to cyber incidents, and minimizing the impact of cyber-attacks.

4.   Best Practices and Strategies:

•   Drawing on case studies and expert insights, the chapter highlights best practices and strategies for building resilient government cyber defences. These include proactive threat intelligence sharing, continuous monitoring and detection, secure-by-design principles, cyber hygiene training, and public-private partnerships. By adopting these best practices, government agencies can enhance their cybersecurity resilience and adaptability in the face of evolving cyber threats.

5.   Challenges and Considerations:

•   Despite the importance of building resilient cyber defences, government agencies face various challenges and considerations in achieving cyber resilience. These include resource constraints, legacy IT systems, complex regulatory environments, workforce shortages, and geopolitical tensions. The chapter examines these challenges and offers recommendations for overcoming them to strengthen government cybersecurity resilience effectively.

6.   International Cooperation and Collaboration:

•   Recognizing that cyber threats are inherently transnational in nature, the chapter emphasizes the importance of international cooperation and collaboration in building resilient government cyber defences. Governments must work together to share threat intelligence, coordinate incident response efforts, harmonize cybersecurity standards, and promote norms of responsible behaviour in cyberspace.

7.   Future Outlook:

•   The chapter concludes by reflecting on the future outlook for building resilient government cyber defences. While cyber threats will continue to evolve and proliferate, governments have the opportunity to enhance their cybersecurity resilience through proactive investments, collaboration, and innovation.

By prioritising cyber resilience and adopting a holistic approach to cybersecurity, governments can better protect their digital infrastructure, preserve national security interests, and promote trust and confidence in government institutions.

Conclusion:

Chapter 4 provides a comprehensive overview of the imperative of building resilient government cyber defences in an increasingly complex and dynamic cyber threat landscape. By understanding the key components of cyber resilience, adopting best practices and strategies, addressing challenges and considerations, and fostering international cooperation, governments can enhance their cybersecurity resilience and adaptability to safeguard national interests and ensure the continuity of government operations in the face of cyber threats.

Frameworks and Best Practices for Developing Cybersecurity Strategies

In an era of increasing cyber threats and vulnerabilities, developing effective cybersecurity strategies is essential for organizations to protect their assets, mitigate risks, and ensure business continuity.

This book explores frameworks and best practices for developing cybersecurity strategies, providing insights into key methodologies, principles, and considerations that organizations can leverage to enhance their cybersecurity posture and resilience.

1. Importance of Cybersecurity Strategies:

• Cybersecurity strategies serve as a roadmap for organizations to identify, assess, and prioritize cyber risks, as well as to define goals, objectives, and action plans for mitigating these risks effectively.

• By developing cybersecurity strategies, organizations can align their cybersecurity efforts with business objectives, allocate resources efficiently, and establish a proactive approach to cybersecurity governance and risk management.

2.   Frameworks for Developing Cybersecurity Strategies:

•   Several frameworks exist to guide organizations in developing cybersecurity strategies, each offering a structured approach to assessing cyber risks, defining security controls, and measuring cybersecurity maturity. Some widely adopted frameworks include:

•   NIST Cybersecurity Framework: Developed by the National Institute of Standards and Technology (NIST), this framework provides a flexible, risk-based approach to managing cybersecurity risks, focusing on five core functions: Identify, Protect, Detect, Respond, and Recover.

•   ISO/IEC 27001: This international standard outlines requirements for establishing, implementing, maintaining, and continually improving an information security management system (ISMS) within an organization, helping organizations manage their information security risks effectively.

• CIS Controls: Developed by the Center for Internet Security (CIS), this framework provides a prioritized set of security controls and best practices for defending against common cyber threats, helping organizations establish a baseline for cybersecurity hygiene.

• COBIT (Control Objectives for Information and Related Technologies): Developed by ISACA, COBIT provides a framework for governing and managing enterprise IT, including cybersecurity governance, risk management, and compliance.

3. Key Components of Cybersecurity Strategies:
   • Regardless of the framework chosen, cybersecurity strategies typically include several key components, such as:

• Risk Assessment: Identifying and assessing cyber risks, threats, and vulnerabilities facing the organization, including risks to data, systems, networks, and assets.

• Governance and Oversight: Establishing clear governance structures, roles, and responsibilities for cybersecurity oversight, accountability, and decision-making.

• Security Controls: Implementing technical, administrative, and physical security controls to protect against identified cyber risks and threats, including access controls, encryption, monitoring, and incident response.

• Incident Response and Recovery: Developing and implementing incident response plans and procedures to detect, respond to, and recover from cybersecurity incidents effectively, minimizing their impact on operations and stakeholders.

• Continuous Improvement: Establishing processes for monitoring, evaluating, and continuously improving cybersecurity posture and resilience over time, adapting to emerging threats and changing business requirements.

4. Best Practices for Developing Cybersecurity Strategies:

•   In addition to following established frameworks, organizations can leverage best practices to enhance the effectiveness and resilience of their cybersecurity strategies, including:

•   Executive Leadership and Buy-in: Securing executive leadership support and buy-in for cybersecurity initiatives, ensuring alignment with business objectives and priorities.

•   Stakeholder Engagement: Engaging stakeholders across the organization, including IT, legal, compliance, risk management, and business units, to ensure a holistic and integrated approach to cybersecurity.

•   Risk-Based Approach: Adopting a risk-based approach to cybersecurity, prioritizing efforts based on the likelihood and impact of potential cyber threats and vulnerabilities.

• Collaboration and Information Sharing: Fostering collaboration and information sharing with industry peers, government agencies, law enforcement, and cybersecurity organizations to enhance situational awareness and collective defence against cyber threats.

• Training and Awareness: Providing cybersecurity training and awareness programs for employees, contractors, and third-party partners to promote a culture of cybersecurity awareness, accountability, and compliance.

• Third-Party Risk Management: Assessing and managing cybersecurity risks associated with third-party vendors, suppliers, and service providers, including due diligence, contract negotiations, and ongoing monitoring.

5. Considerations for Developing Cybersecurity Strategies:

• When developing cybersecurity strategies, organizations should consider several key factors, including:

- Business Objectives and Risk Appetite: Aligning cybersecurity strategies with business objectives, risk tolerance, and regulatory requirements to ensure a balanced and cost-effective approach to managing cyber risks.

- Industry Regulations and Compliance: Understanding industry-specific regulations, standards, and compliance requirements, and integrating them into cybersecurity strategies to ensure legal and regulatory compliance.

- Emerging Threat Landscape: Staying abreast of emerging cyber threats, trends, and tactics, and adjusting cybersecurity strategies accordingly to address evolving risks and vulnerabilities.

- Resource Allocation and Budgeting: Allocating resources, budget, and personnel effectively to support cybersecurity initiatives and priorities, balancing investments in prevention, detection, and response capabilities.

• Organizational Culture and Maturity: Assessing organizational culture, maturity, and readiness for cybersecurity initiatives, and tailoring strategies and approaches to fit the organization's unique context and capabilities.

Conclusion:

In conclusion, developing effective cybersecurity strategies is crucial for organizations to protect against cyber threats, mitigate risks, and ensure business resilience in an increasingly digitalized and interconnected world. By leveraging established frameworks, adopting best practices, and considering key factors and considerations, organizations can develop robust and resilient cybersecurity strategies that align with business objectives, address regulatory requirements, and adapt to emerging cyber threats and challenges.

By taking a proactive and risk-based approach to cybersecurity strategy development, organizations can enhance their cybersecurity posture, strengthen defences, and safeguard their digital assets and operations against evolving cyber threats.

Importance of Collaboration and Information Sharing Among Government Departments

In the face of evolving and complex cyber threats, collaboration and information sharing among government departments are essential for effective cybersecurity defence.

As cyber-attacks become increasingly sophisticated and targeted, no single government agency can address the breadth and depth of cyber risks alone. This book explores the importance of collaboration and information sharing among government departments in the context of cybersecurity, highlighting the benefits, challenges, and best practices for fostering a culture of cooperation and coordination.

1. Enhanced Situational Awareness:

•   Collaboration and information sharing enable government departments to gain a comprehensive understanding of the cyber threat landscape, including emerging threats, trends, and tactics.

• By pooling resources, expertise, and intelligence, government agencies can enhance situational awareness, identify potential vulnerabilities, and prioritize response efforts to address the most critical cyber risks effectively.

2. Coordinated Response to Cyber Incidents:

• In the event of a cyber incident, timely and coordinated response is crucial for minimizing damage, containing the threat, and restoring operations.

• Collaboration among government departments facilitates a coordinated response framework, enabling swift sharing of threat intelligence, coordination of incident response activities, and deployment of resources to mitigate the impact of cyber-attacks.

3.   Leveraging Specialized Expertise and Resources:

•   Government departments often possess specialized expertise, resources, and capabilities that can complement each other in addressing different aspects of cybersecurity.

•   By collaborating, departments can leverage each other's strengths, such as law enforcement's investigative capabilities, intelligence agencies' threat analysis expertise, and regulatory agencies' compliance oversight, to enhance overall cybersecurity resilience.

4.   Strengthening Cybersecurity Governance and Policy:

•   Collaboration among government departments is essential for developing coherent cybersecurity governance frameworks, policies, and regulations that address the diverse needs and priorities of different sectors and stakeholders.

•   By working together, departments can harmonize cybersecurity standards, regulations, and best practices, promote consistency and interoperability, and ensure alignment with national cybersecurity objectives and strategies.

5.   Promoting Cross-Agency Information Sharing Platforms:

•   Establishing cross-agency information sharing platforms and mechanisms is critical for facilitating seamless exchange of threat intelligence, incident data, and best practices among government departments.

•   These platforms can take various forms, including information sharing centres, fusion centres, threat intelligence platforms, and collaborative working groups, providing a secure and trusted environment for sharing sensitive information.

6.   Overcoming Challenges and Barriers:

•   While collaboration and information sharing offer numerous benefits, they also present challenges and barriers that must be addressed to maximize their effectiveness.

• Challenges include concerns about information security and confidentiality, bureaucratic hurdles, cultural differences, legal and regulatory constraints, and resource constraints.

• Overcoming these challenges requires building trust and confidence among stakeholders, establishing clear policies and protocols for information sharing, addressing legal and regulatory barriers, and fostering a culture of collaboration and cooperation.

7. Best Practices for Collaboration and Information Sharing:

• To promote effective collaboration and information sharing among government departments, several best practices can be adopted:

• Establish clear roles, responsibilities, and governance structures for coordinating cybersecurity efforts.

• Foster a culture of trust, transparency, and mutual respect among stakeholders.

• Provide training and resources to enhance cybersecurity awareness and skills across departments.

• Develop standardized protocols and procedures for sharing threat intelligence and incident data.

• Encourage participation in cross-agency working groups, exercises, and tabletop simulations to build relationships and enhance coordination.

Conclusion:

In conclusion, collaboration and information sharing among government departments are essential pillars of effective cybersecurity defence in an increasingly interconnected and digitized world.

By working together, departments can enhance situational awareness, coordinate response efforts, leverage specialized expertise and resources, strengthen cybersecurity governance, and promote a culture of collaboration and cooperation. Despite challenges and barriers, adopting best practices and fostering a collaborative mindset can help overcome obstacles and build a resilient cybersecurity ecosystem that protects national interests, critical infrastructure, and citizen welfare against evolving cyber threats.

Capacity Building and Training Initiatives for Government Employees

In today's digital age, government employees play a crucial role in defending against cyber threats, safeguarding sensitive information, and ensuring the resilience of government operations. However, the rapid evolution of cyber threats and technologies requires continuous learning and upskilling to keep pace with emerging challenges.

This book explores the importance of capacity building and training initiatives for government employees in the context of cybersecurity, highlighting the benefits, challenges, and best practices for enhancing cyber resilience across government agencies.

1. Importance of Capacity Building and Training:

• Government employees are often targeted by cyber attackers seeking to exploit human vulnerabilities, such as phishing scams, social engineering attacks, and insider threats.

• Capacity building and training initiatives help government employees develop the knowledge, skills, and awareness necessary to recognize and respond to cyber threats effectively, reducing the likelihood of successful cyber-attacks and mitigating their impact.

2. Building Cybersecurity Awareness:

• One of the primary objectives of capacity building and training initiatives is to raise cybersecurity awareness among government employees, ensuring they understand the importance of cybersecurity, their roles and responsibilities in protecting government assets, and the potential consequences of cyber threats.

• Training programs cover topics such as cyber hygiene best practices, password security, email security, social engineering awareness, and incident reporting procedures, empowering employees to make informed decisions and adopt secure behaviours in their day-to-day activities.

3.   Developing Technical Skills:

•   In addition to cybersecurity awareness, capacity building and training initiatives focus on developing technical skills and expertise among government employees, particularly those responsible for managing and securing IT systems and networks.

•   Training programs cover a range of technical topics, including network security, endpoint protection, encryption, vulnerability management, incident response, and threat intelligence analysis, equipping employees with the knowledge and tools needed to detect, analyse, and mitigate cyber threats effectively.

4.   Enhancing Incident Response Capabilities:

•   Capacity building and training initiatives also aim to enhance incident response capabilities within government agencies, ensuring employees are prepared to respond effectively to cyber incidents and minimize their impact on operations.

• Incident response training covers topics such as incident detection and triage, containment and mitigation strategies, evidence collection and preservation, communication and coordination protocols, and post-incident analysis and reporting, enabling employees to respond swiftly and decisively to cyber incidents.

5. Promoting a Culture of Cybersecurity:

• Capacity building and training initiatives play a vital role in promoting a culture of cybersecurity within government agencies, fostering a shared understanding of cybersecurity risks and responsibilities among employees at all levels of the organization.

• By promoting a culture of cybersecurity, training programs encourage collaboration, communication, and accountability, empowering employees to take ownership of cybersecurity and contribute to a more resilient and secure government environment.

6.   Challenges and Considerations:

•   Despite the importance of capacity building and training initiatives, several challenges and considerations must be addressed to maximize their effectiveness:

•   Limited Resources: Government agencies may face constraints in terms of budget, time, and personnel for developing and delivering training programs.

•   Technical Complexity: Cybersecurity is a rapidly evolving and complex field, requiring continuous learning and adaptation to keep pace with emerging threats and technologies.

•   Cultural Resistance: Some employees may resist cybersecurity training initiatives due to perceived inconvenience, lack of awareness, or scepticism about the relevance of cybersecurity to their roles.

•   Compliance Requirements: Government agencies must comply with various regulatory requirements and standards for cybersecurity training, which may impose additional burdens and constraints on training programs.

7.   Best Practices for Capacity Building and Training:

•   To overcome challenges and maximize the effectiveness of capacity building and training initiatives, government agencies can adopt several best practices:

•   Develop a comprehensive training strategy aligned with organizational goals, priorities, and regulatory requirements.

•   Utilize a variety of training delivery methods, including in-person workshops, online courses, webinars, simulations, and tabletop exercises, to accommodate different learning styles and preferences.

•   Tailor training programs to the specific needs and roles of employees, providing targeted training for IT professionals, managers, executives, and frontline staff.

• Incorporate real-world scenarios, case studies, and practical exercises into training programs to reinforce learning and encourage hands-on experience.

• Evaluate training effectiveness through pre-and post-training assessments, surveys, and feedback mechanisms, and continuously iterate and improve training programs based on feedback and performance metrics.

Conclusion:

Capacity building and training initiatives are essential for enhancing cyber resilience and empowering government employees to effectively defend against cyber threats. By raising cybersecurity awareness, developing technical skills, enhancing incident response capabilities, and promoting a culture of cybersecurity, training programs enable government agencies to build a workforce that is vigilant, knowledgeable, and prepared to confront the evolving cybersecurity landscape.

Despite challenges, adopting best practices and investing in ongoing training and development is critical for ensuring the effectiveness and sustainability of cybersecurity initiatives within government agencies, ultimately contributing to a more secure and resilient government ecosystem.

Chapter 5: Securing Critical Government Assets

Securing critical government assets is paramount to maintaining national security, protecting sensitive information, and ensuring the continuity of government operations. As government agencies increasingly rely on digital systems and technologies to deliver essential services and conduct operations, the protection of critical assets from cyber threats becomes even more critical. This chapter explores the challenges, strategies, and best practices for securing critical government assets, including infrastructure, data, and systems, against cyber threats.

1.   Importance of Securing Critical Government Assets:

•   Critical government assets encompass a wide range of physical and digital assets, including critical infrastructure (e.g., energy, transportation, water), sensitive information (e.g., classified data, citizen records), and essential systems and services (e.g., communication networks, emergency response).

- Securing these assets is essential to safeguarding national security, preserving public trust, and ensuring the resilience of government operations in the face of cyber threats, natural disasters, and other disruptions.

2. Identifying Critical Assets and Risks:

- The first step in securing critical government assets is to identify and prioritize critical assets and associated risks. This involves conducting comprehensive risk assessments to identify vulnerabilities, threats, and potential consequences of cyber-attacks on critical assets.

- Critical assets may include physical infrastructure, such as power plants, transportation systems, and government facilities, as well as digital assets, such as sensitive data repositories, communication networks, and operational systems.

3.   Developing Risk-Based Security Strategies:

•   Based on the identified risks and critical assets,
government agencies can develop risk-based security
strategies to mitigate cyber threats and vulnerabilities
effectively.

•   Security strategies should prioritize the protection of
critical assets based on their importance to national
security, economic stability, public safety, and continuity
of government operations.

•   Strategies may include implementing multi-layered
security controls, access controls, encryption,
monitoring, and incident response capabilities to protect
critical assets from cyber threats.

4.   Enhancing Security Posture:

•   Securing critical government assets requires a multifaceted approach that encompasses technical,
administrative, and physical security measures.

- Technical security measures may include network segmentation, firewalls, intrusion detection systems (IDS), antivirus software, and encryption to protect data and systems from unauthorized access and cyber-attacks.

- Administrative security measures involve implementing policies, procedures, and controls to govern access to critical assets, manage user privileges, and enforce security best practices across government agencies.

- Physical security measures may include access controls, surveillance, perimeter security, and disaster recovery plans to protect physical infrastructure and assets from physical and cyber threats.

5. Implementing Cyber Hygiene Practices:

- Maintaining good cyber hygiene practices is essential for securing critical government assets and reducing the risk of cyber-attacks.

- Cyber hygiene practices include regular software patching and updates, strong password management, user training and awareness, secure configuration management, and vulnerability scanning and remediation.

- By adopting and enforcing cyber hygiene practices, government agencies can reduce the likelihood of successful cyber-attacks and minimize the impact of security incidents on critical assets.

6. Collaboration and Information Sharing:

- Collaboration and information sharing among government agencies, industry partners, and international allies are essential for securing critical government assets effectively.

- Sharing threat intelligence, best practices, and lessons learned enables government agencies to stay ahead of emerging cyber threats, identify vulnerabilities, and strengthen their security posture.

• Collaboration also facilitates coordinated incident response efforts, enabling government agencies to respond swiftly and effectively to cyber incidents that may impact critical assets.

7. Investing in Emerging Technologies:

• Investing in emerging technologies, such as artificial intelligence (AI), machine learning (ML), and blockchain, can enhance the security of critical government assets by enabling advanced threat detection, anomaly detection, and encryption.

• AI and ML technologies can analyse large volumes of data to identify patterns and anomalies indicative of cyber threats, while blockchain technology can provide tamper-proof and transparent record-keeping for critical transactions and data exchanges.

Conclusion:

Securing critical government assets is a complex and multifaceted challenge that requires a coordinated and proactive approach. By identifying and prioritizing critical assets, developing risk-based security strategies, enhancing security posture, implementing cyber hygiene practices, fostering collaboration and information sharing, and investing in emerging technologies, government agencies can strengthen the security of critical assets and protect national security, public trust, and the continuity of government operations.

Despite the evolving nature of cyber threats, adopting a comprehensive and adaptive security approach can help government agencies stay ahead of emerging risks and ensure the resilience of critical government assets in an increasingly digitalized world.

Protecting Government Networks, Systems, and Data

Government networks, systems, and data are prime targets for cyber-attacks due to their critical role in national security, public safety, and the delivery of essential services. Securing government assets against cyber threats requires a comprehensive and multi-layered approach that encompasses technical, administrative, and physical security measures. This book explores the challenges, strategies, and best practices for protecting government networks, systems, and data from cyber threats, with a focus on ensuring the confidentiality, integrity, and availability of sensitive information and critical infrastructure.

1.   Understanding the Threat Landscape:

•   Government networks and systems face a diverse range of cyber threats, including malware, ransomware, phishing attacks, insider threats, and nation-state-sponsored cyber espionage.

•   Cyber adversaries target government assets to steal sensitive information, disrupt operations, undermine public trust, and compromise national security interests.

2.   Securing Government Networks:

•   Government networks are the backbone of digital communication, collaboration, and information exchange within and across government agencies.

- Securing government networks involves implementing robust technical controls, such as firewalls, intrusion detection systems (IDS), intrusion prevention systems (IPS), and virtual private networks (VPNs), to protect against unauthorized access, malware, and other cyber threats.

- Network segmentation, encryption, access controls, and continuous monitoring are essential for protecting government networks from internal and external cyber threats.

3. Protecting Government Systems:

- Government systems, including servers, databases, and endpoints, are primary targets for cyber-attacks seeking to compromise sensitive data, disrupt operations, or gain unauthorized access to critical infrastructure.

- Securing government systems requires implementing strong authentication mechanisms, patch management processes, endpoint protection solutions, and secure

116

configuration management practices to mitigate vulnerabilities and prevent unauthorized access.

• Regular vulnerability scanning, penetration testing, and security audits are essential for identifying and addressing security gaps in government systems proactively.

4. Safeguarding Government Data:

• Government data, including classified information, citizen records, and intellectual property, must be protected against unauthorized access, disclosure, alteration, or destruction.

• Implementing data encryption, access controls, data loss prevention (DLP) solutions, and data backup and recovery processes are critical for safeguarding government data from cyber threats and ensuring data confidentiality and integrity.

• Data classification, data retention policies, and secure data disposal practices help government agencies manage and protect sensitive information throughout its lifecycle.

5.   Enhancing Insider Threat Detection:

•   Insider threats pose a significant risk to government networks, systems, and data, as malicious insiders or negligent employees may intentionally or inadvertently compromise security.

•   Implementing user behaviour analytics (UBA), privileged access management (PAM), and insider threat detection solutions can help government agencies detect and mitigate insider threats by monitoring user activities, identifying anomalous behaviour, and enforcing least privilege access controls.

6.   Strengthening Incident Response Capabilities:

•   Despite preventive measures, government agencies must be prepared to respond swiftly and effectively to cyber incidents that may compromise network security, disrupt operations, or compromise sensitive data.

•   Establishing incident response plans, procedures, and communication protocols, conducting regular incident response drills and tabletop exercises, and establishing partnerships with law enforcement and cybersecurity organizations are essential for enhancing incident response capabilities and minimizing the impact of cyber incidents.

7.   Promoting Cybersecurity Awareness and Training:

•   Government employees are often the weakest link in cybersecurity defences, as human error and lack of awareness can inadvertently expose government networks, systems, and data to cyber threats.

•   Providing regular cybersecurity awareness training, phishing simulations, and role-based security training for employees, contractors, and third-party partners can help raise awareness of cybersecurity risks, promote secure behaviours, and reduce the likelihood of successful cyber-attacks.

8. Collaboration and Information Sharing:

• Collaboration and information sharing among government agencies, industry partners, and international allies are essential for identifying emerging cyber threats, sharing threat intelligence, and coordinating incident response efforts.

• Establishing trusted information sharing platforms, participating in information sharing communities and consortia, and collaborating on joint cybersecurity exercises and initiatives help government agencies stay ahead of evolving cyber threats and enhance collective defence against cyber-attacks.

Conclusion:

Protecting government networks, systems, and data is a complex and ongoing endeavour that requires a combination of technical controls, administrative policies, and user awareness initiatives. By implementing robust security measures, enhancing incident response capabilities, promoting cybersecurity awareness and training, and fostering collaboration and information sharing, government agencies can strengthen their cyber defences, mitigate cyber risks, and safeguard national security, public trust, and the continuity of government operations against evolving cyber threats. Despite the challenges posed by cyber adversaries, a proactive and collaborative approach to cybersecurity can help government agencies stay resilient and adaptive in the face of emerging cyber threats.

Strategies for Securing Critical Infrastructure and Public Services

Critical infrastructure and public services are the backbone of modern society, providing essential functions that support economic prosperity, public safety, and quality of life. However, they are also prime targets for cyber-attacks, as disruption or compromise of critical infrastructure can have far-reaching consequences, including economic disruption, loss of life, and national security threats. This book explores strategies for securing critical infrastructure and public services against cyber threats, focusing on proactive measures to enhance resilience, mitigate risks, and ensure the continuity of essential functions.

1. Understanding Critical Infrastructure:

• Critical infrastructure encompasses a wide range of sectors, including energy, transportation, water, healthcare, telecommunications, finance, and government services.

• Critical infrastructure is characterized by its importance to the functioning of society and the economy, as well as its interdependence with other sectors and its vulnerability to various threats, including cyber-attacks.

2. Identifying Vulnerabilities and Risks:

• The first step in securing critical infrastructure is to identify and assess vulnerabilities and risks that may compromise its integrity, availability, or confidentiality.

• Vulnerabilities may arise from outdated or insecure technology, lack of security controls, insufficient resilience measures, or human error, while risks may stem from cyber threats, natural disasters, physical attacks, or supply chain disruptions.

3. Adopting a Risk-Based Approach:

• Securing critical infrastructure requires a risk-based approach that prioritizes efforts based on the likelihood and potential impact of identified risks.

• Risk assessment and management processes help identify critical assets, assess their vulnerability to cyber threats, prioritize security controls and investments, and develop risk mitigation strategies tailored to specific threats and scenarios.

4. Implementing Multilayered Security Controls:

• Securing critical infrastructure involves implementing multilayered security controls that protect against a wide range of cyber threats and attack vectors.

• Technical controls, such as firewalls, intrusion detection systems (IDS), intrusion prevention systems (IPS), antivirus software, and encryption, help detect, prevent, and mitigate cyber-attacks targeting critical infrastructure systems and networks.

• Physical security measures, such as access controls, surveillance cameras, perimeter fencing, and security guards, help protect physical infrastructure from unauthorized access, sabotage, or tampering.

5. Enhancing Resilience and Redundancy:

• Enhancing resilience and redundancy is essential for ensuring the continuity of critical infrastructure and public services in the face of cyber-attacks, natural disasters, or other disruptions.

• Redundant systems, backup power sources, alternate communication channels, and disaster recovery plans help minimize the impact of disruptions and ensure the timely restoration of essential functions.

• Continuous monitoring, incident response plans, and regular drills and exercises help maintain readiness and preparedness to respond to cyber incidents and other emergencies effectively.

6. Promoting Public-Private Partnerships:

• Securing critical infrastructure requires collaboration and partnership between government agencies, private sector entities, industry associations, and international partners.

• Public-private partnerships enable information sharing, threat intelligence sharing, joint risk assessments, and coordinated response efforts, fostering a collective defence approach to securing critical infrastructure and public services.

• Collaboration between government and industry stakeholders helps leverage resources, expertise, and best practices to address shared cyber threats and vulnerabilities effectively.

7. Investing in Emerging Technologies:

•   Investing in emerging technologies, such as artificial intelligence (AI), machine learning (ML), blockchain, and the Internet of Things (IoT), can enhance the security and resilience of critical infrastructure and public services.

•   AI and ML technologies enable advanced threat detection, anomaly detection, and predictive analytics, helping identify and respond to cyber threats in real-time.

•   Blockchain technology provides tamper-proof and transparent record-keeping for critical transactions and data exchanges, enhancing data integrity and trust in critical infrastructure systems.

8. Enhancing Cybersecurity Awareness and Training:

•   Securing critical infrastructure requires a knowledgeable and skilled workforce that is aware of cyber threats, understands security best practices, and can respond effectively to cyber incidents.

- Providing cybersecurity awareness training, technical training, and incident response training for employees, contractors, and third-party partners helps promote a culture of cybersecurity and ensure all stakeholders are prepared to defend against cyber threats.

Conclusion:

Securing critical infrastructure and public services is a complex and multifaceted challenge that requires a coordinated and proactive approach. By identifying vulnerabilities and risks, adopting a risk-based approach to security, implementing multilayered security controls, enhancing resilience and redundancy, promoting public-private partnerships, investing in emerging technologies, and enhancing cybersecurity awareness and training, organizations can strengthen the security and resilience of critical infrastructure and public services against cyber threats.

Despite the evolving nature of cyber threats, a proactive and collaborative approach to cybersecurity can help ensure the continuity of essential functions, protect national security, and safeguard the well-being and prosperity of society as a whole.

Importance of Incident Response and Recovery Planning

In today's digital landscape, cyber incidents are an unfortunate reality for organizations of all sizes and sectors. These incidents can range from data breaches and ransomware attacks to system outages and insider threats, causing significant disruption, financial loss, and reputational damage.

Incident response and recovery planning are critical components of cybersecurity strategy, enabling organizations to effectively detect, respond to, and recover from cyber incidents. This book explores the importance of incident response and recovery planning, highlighting the benefits, key components, and best practices for organizations in mitigating the impact of cyber threats.

1. Proactive Detection and Response:

•   Incident response and recovery planning enable organizations to adopt a proactive approach to cybersecurity, allowing them to detect and respond to cyber incidents in a timely and effective manner.

•   By implementing incident response plans and procedures, organizations can establish clear roles, responsibilities, and communication channels for incident detection, reporting, escalation, and resolution, minimizing the time to detect and respond to cyber threats.

2. Minimizing Downtime and Disruption:

•   Cyber incidents can cause significant downtime and disruption to business operations, resulting in financial losses, productivity declines, and damage to customer trust and reputation.

•   Incident response and recovery planning help organizations minimize the impact of cyber incidents by implementing strategies and measures to restore operations, mitigate damage, and maintain business continuity in the event of an incident.

3.   Limiting Financial Losses:

•   Cyber incidents can have significant financial implications for organizations, including direct costs associated with incident response, remediation, and recovery efforts, as well as indirect costs stemming from lost revenue, legal liabilities, regulatory fines, and reputational damage.

•   Effective incident response and recovery planning can help organizations mitigate financial losses by enabling swift and efficient response to cyber incidents, reducing the duration and severity of disruptions, and minimizing the associated costs.

4.   Protecting Sensitive Information:

•   Cyber incidents often involve the compromise of sensitive information, such as customer data, intellectual property, and proprietary business information, which can have serious consequences for organizations, including regulatory penalties, legal liabilities, and loss of trust and confidence from stakeholders.

• Incident response and recovery planning help organizations protect sensitive information by implementing measures to prevent unauthorized access, contain breaches, and mitigate the impact of data exfiltration or leakage.

5. Maintaining Regulatory Compliance:

• Many industries are subject to regulatory requirements and data protection laws that mandate organizations to implement incident response and recovery plans to protect sensitive information and respond effectively to cyber incidents.

• Incident response and recovery planning help organizations maintain regulatory compliance by establishing processes and procedures for incident detection, reporting, investigation, and notification, as required by applicable regulations and standards.

6.   Enhancing Stakeholder Trust and Confidence:

• In today's interconnected and data-driven world, stakeholders, including customers, partners, investors, and regulators, expect organizations to have robust cybersecurity measures in place to protect their data and ensure the integrity and availability of critical services.

• Incident response and recovery planning demonstrate an organization's commitment to cybersecurity and resilience, enhancing stakeholder trust and confidence in its ability to effectively respond to cyber threats and safeguard their interests.

7.   Improving Organizational Resilience:

• Cyber incidents are inevitable, but organizations can improve their resilience and ability to recover from such incidents by implementing incident response and recovery planning.

• Incident response and recovery planning help organizations develop the capabilities, processes, and resources necessary to effectively respond to cyber incidents, learn from past incidents, and continuously improve their cybersecurity posture over time.

8. Best Practices for Incident Response and Recovery Planning:

•   Develop a comprehensive incident response plan that outlines roles, responsibilities, and procedures for incident detection, reporting, analysis, containment, eradication, recovery, and post-incident review.

•   Establish clear communication channels and escalation procedures to ensure timely reporting and coordination of incident response efforts across relevant stakeholders.

•   Conduct regular training and exercises to ensure that employees, contractors, and third-party partners are familiar with their roles and responsibilities in the event of a cyber incident.

•   Maintain an inventory of critical assets, including systems, applications, data, and personnel, and prioritize their protection based on their importance to business operations and regulatory requirements.

• Implement monitoring and detection capabilities, such as intrusion detection systems (IDS), security information and event management (SIEM) systems, and endpoint detection and response (EDR) solutions, to detect and alert on suspicious activities and potential security breaches.

• Establish relationships with external stakeholders, such as law enforcement agencies, incident response firms, and industry information sharing organizations, to facilitate collaboration and information sharing during incident response and recovery efforts.

Conclusion:

Incident response and recovery planning are critical components of effective cybersecurity strategy, enabling organizations to detect, respond to, and recover from cyber incidents in a timely and effective manner. By implementing proactive measures to detect and respond to cyber threats, minimizing downtime and disruption, limiting financial losses, protecting sensitive information, maintaining regulatory compliance, enhancing stakeholder trust and confidence, and improving organizational resilience, organizations can mitigate the impact of cyber incidents and safeguard their business operations, reputation, and bottom line.

Despite the evolving nature of cyber threats, investing in incident response and recovery planning is essential for organizations to effectively manage cyber risks and maintain business continuity in today's digital landscape.

Chapter 6: Compliance and Regulatory Frameworks

In today's interconnected and data-driven world, organizations are subject to a myriad of compliance requirements and regulatory frameworks designed to protect sensitive information, safeguard consumer privacy, and ensure the integrity and security of digital assets.

Compliance and regulatory frameworks play a crucial role in guiding organizations' cybersecurity efforts, providing standards, guidelines, and best practices for managing cyber risks and mitigating the impact of cyber threats. This chapter explores the importance of compliance and regulatory frameworks in cybersecurity, highlighting their impact on organizations, key components, and best practices for achieving compliance.

1. Importance of Compliance and Regulatory Frameworks:

•   Compliance and regulatory frameworks are essential for promoting cybersecurity best practices, ensuring legal and regulatory compliance, and protecting organizations from cyber threats and liabilities.

•   Regulatory compliance helps organizations demonstrate due diligence in managing cyber risks, mitigate legal and financial liabilities, and maintain trust and confidence among stakeholders, including customers, partners, investors, and regulators.

2. Impact on Organizations:

•   Compliance and regulatory frameworks have a significant impact on organizations across industries, requiring them to implement specific cybersecurity measures, policies, and procedures to protect sensitive information and maintain regulatory compliance.

•   Non-compliance with regulatory requirements can result in severe consequences for organizations, including regulatory fines, legal liabilities, reputational damage, loss of customer trust, and business disruption.

3. Key Components of Compliance and Regulatory Frameworks:

• Compliance and regulatory frameworks typically include a set of standards, guidelines, and requirements that organizations must adhere to in order to achieve compliance.

• Key components of compliance and regulatory frameworks may include data protection regulations, industry-specific standards (e.g., PCI DSS for payment card industry, HIPAA for healthcare industry), international standards (e.g., ISO 27001 for information security management), and government regulations (e.g., GDPR in the European Union, CCPA in California).

4. Achieving Compliance:

• Achieving compliance with regulatory frameworks requires organizations to implement a range of cybersecurity measures, policies, and controls designed to protect sensitive information, mitigate cyber risks, and ensure regulatory compliance.

• Common cybersecurity measures and controls include data encryption, access controls, network segmentation, vulnerability management, incident response planning, and employee training and awareness.

5. Best Practices for Compliance:

• To achieve compliance with regulatory frameworks effectively, organizations can follow several best practices:

• Conduct regular risk assessments to identify cybersecurity risks and vulnerabilities.

• Implement cybersecurity policies and procedures that align with regulatory requirements and industry best practices.

- Deploy technical controls and security solutions to protect sensitive data, detect and respond to cyber threats, and ensure the integrity and availability of critical systems and information.

- Monitor and audit cybersecurity controls and processes to ensure ongoing compliance with regulatory requirements and identify areas for improvement.

- Provide training and awareness programs to educate employees, contractors, and third-party partners about cybersecurity risks, responsibilities, and compliance requirements.

- Establish incident response and recovery plans to effectively respond to cybersecurity incidents and minimize their impact on business operations and regulatory compliance.

6. Continuous Compliance Monitoring and Improvement:

- Achieving compliance is not a one-time effort but an ongoing process that requires continuous monitoring, assessment, and improvement of cybersecurity practices and controls.

• Organizations should regularly review and update their cybersecurity policies, procedures, and controls to reflect changes in regulatory requirements, emerging cyber threats, and business needs.

• Continuous compliance monitoring helps organizations identify and address gaps in cybersecurity practices, mitigate new and evolving cyber risks, and maintain compliance with regulatory requirements over time.

7.   Collaboration and Information Sharing:

• Collaboration and information sharing among organizations, industry associations, and regulatory authorities are essential for promoting cybersecurity best practices, sharing threat intelligence, and addressing common cybersecurity challenges.

• Participating in industry forums, information sharing communities, and collaborative initiatives enables organizations to stay informed about emerging cyber threats, share lessons learned, and benchmark their cybersecurity practices against industry peers.

Conclusion:

Compliance and regulatory frameworks play a crucial role in guiding organizations' cybersecurity efforts, providing standards, guidelines, and requirements for managing cyber risks and protecting sensitive information. By achieving compliance with regulatory frameworks, organizations can demonstrate their commitment to cybersecurity best practices, mitigate legal and financial liabilities, and maintain trust and confidence among stakeholders.

However, achieving compliance is not a one-time effort but an ongoing process that requires continuous monitoring, assessment, and improvement of cybersecurity practices and controls. By following best practices for compliance, organizations can effectively manage cyber risks, protect sensitive information, and maintain regulatory compliance in today's complex and evolving cybersecurity landscape.

Overview of Existing Cybersecurity Laws and Regulations in African Countries

The digital revolution has transformed the way people communicate, conduct business, and access information across the globe, including in African countries. With increased connectivity comes greater risks of cyber threats and attacks, prompting governments across Africa to enact cybersecurity laws and regulations to protect their citizens, critical infrastructure, and digital assets.

This book provides an overview of existing cybersecurity laws and regulations in African countries, highlighting key provisions, challenges, and future trends in cybersecurity legislation.

1.   The Need for Cybersecurity Legislation in Africa:

•   The rapid expansion of digital technology in Africa has led to increased cyber threats, including cybercrime, data breaches, and malicious cyber activities.

- Cybersecurity legislation is essential for protecting critical infrastructure, safeguarding personal and sensitive information, and combating cybercrime, fraud, and other cyber threats in African countries.

2. Overview of Cybersecurity Laws and Regulations:

- Several African countries have enacted cybersecurity laws and regulations to address the growing cyber threats and protect their digital ecosystems.

- Examples of cybersecurity laws and regulations in African countries include data protection laws, cybercrime laws, national cybersecurity strategies, and sector-specific regulations for industries such as banking, telecommunications, and e-commerce.

3. Key Provisions of Cybersecurity Laws and Regulations:

- Cybersecurity laws and regulations in African countries typically include provisions related to the protection of personal data, prevention of cybercrime, establishment of cybersecurity frameworks and agencies, and promotion of cybersecurity awareness and capacity building.

• Data protection laws often require organizations to implement security measures to protect personal data, obtain consent from individuals for data processing, and notify authorities and affected individuals in the event of a data breach.

• Cybercrime laws criminalize various cyber activities, such as unauthorized access to computer systems, data theft, hacking, malware distribution, and online fraud, and prescribe penalties for offenders.

• National cybersecurity strategies outline the government's approach to cybersecurity, including goals, objectives, priorities, and initiatives for enhancing cybersecurity resilience, promoting information sharing, and building cybersecurity capabilities.

• Sector-specific regulations may impose additional cybersecurity requirements on organizations operating in critical sectors, such as banking, healthcare, energy, and telecommunications, to protect critical infrastructure and sensitive information.

4.   Challenges in Implementing Cybersecurity Laws:
•   Despite the enactment of cybersecurity laws and regulations, African countries face several challenges in implementing and enforcing them effectively.

•   Limited resources, including funding, technical expertise, and institutional capacity, pose challenges to the development and implementation of cybersecurity laws and regulations in African countries.

•   Legal and regulatory frameworks may lag behind technological developments, making it difficult to address emerging cyber threats and regulate new technologies such as artificial intelligence, blockchain, and the Internet of Things (IoT).

•   Cross-border cyber threats and jurisdictional challenges complicate the enforcement of cybersecurity laws, particularly in cases involving cybercrime, data breaches, and international cooperation.

5.   Future Trends in Cybersecurity Legislation:

•   As cyber threats continue to evolve, African countries are likely to strengthen their cybersecurity laws and regulations to address emerging challenges and protect their digital economies.

•   Future trends in cybersecurity legislation may include the adoption of comprehensive data protection laws, the establishment of national cybersecurity agencies and incident response capabilities, and the development of regional and international cooperation frameworks for addressing cross-border cyber threats.

•   African countries may also prioritize cybersecurity capacity building, awareness raising, and public-private partnerships to enhance cybersecurity resilience and promote a culture of cybersecurity across society.

Conclusion:

Cybersecurity laws and regulations play a crucial role in protecting individuals, organizations, and critical infrastructure from cyber threats and ensuring the integrity, confidentiality, and availability of digital assets. In African countries, the enactment and implementation of cybersecurity legislation are essential for addressing the growing cyber threats, promoting trust and confidence in digital technologies, and fostering economic growth and innovation.

Despite challenges in implementation and enforcement, African countries are poised to strengthen their cybersecurity laws and regulations to meet the evolving cyber threat landscape and protect their digital ecosystems in the years to come.

Importance of Compliance and Standards for Government Departments

Government departments play a crucial role in ensuring the delivery of public services, safeguarding citizens' rights, and upholding the rule of law. In today's digital age, where governments increasingly rely on technology to streamline operations and deliver services, compliance with regulatory standards and adherence to established best practices are essential for ensuring the security, integrity, and reliability of government systems and processes.

This book explores the importance of compliance and standards for government departments, highlighting their role in promoting good governance, protecting sensitive information, and enhancing public trust and confidence.

1.   Upholding Legal and Regulatory Requirements:

•   Government departments are subject to a wide range of legal and regulatory requirements governing various aspects of their operations, including data protection, privacy, security, accessibility, and transparency.

•   Compliance with legal and regulatory requirements is essential for government departments to uphold the rule of law, protect citizens' rights, and ensure accountability and transparency in government activities.

2. Protecting Sensitive Information:

• Government departments handle vast amounts of sensitive information, including citizens' personal data, financial records, and national security information, which must be protected from unauthorized access, disclosure, or misuse.

• Compliance with data protection laws and standards, such as GDPR, HIPAA, and PCI DSS, helps government departments safeguard sensitive information, mitigate the risk of data breaches, and maintain the trust and confidence of citizens.

3. Ensuring Cybersecurity and Resilience:

• Government departments are prime targets for cyber-attacks, as they store a wealth of valuable information and provide critical services to citizens.

• Compliance with cybersecurity standards and best practices, such as ISO 27001, NIST Cybersecurity Framework, and CIS Controls, helps government departments strengthen their cybersecurity posture, detect and respond to cyber threats, and ensure the continuity of government operations in the face of cyber-attacks.

4.   Promoting Efficiency and Effectiveness:

•   Compliance with standards and best practices helps government departments streamline their operations, improve efficiency, and enhance service delivery to citizens.

•   Standards such as ITIL (Information Technology Infrastructure Library) and COBIT (Control Objectives for Information and Related Technologies) provide guidelines and best practices for managing IT services and governance, enabling government departments to optimize their IT infrastructure and processes to meet business objectives.

5.   Enhancing Public Trust and Confidence:

•   Compliance with standards and regulations demonstrates a government department's commitment to accountability, transparency, and good governance, enhancing public trust and confidence in its operations.

• By adhering to established standards and best practices, government departments can reassure citizens that their data is being handled responsibly, their rights are being respected, and their interests are being protected.

6. Facilitating Interoperability and Collaboration:

• Compliance with standards promotes interoperability and collaboration among government departments, enabling seamless integration of systems and data sharing across agencies.

• Standards such as XML, SOAP, and REST facilitate the exchange of data and information between government systems, enabling interoperability and collaboration in service delivery and decision-making.

7.   Mitigating Legal and Financial Risks:

•   Non-compliance with regulatory requirements and industry standards can expose government departments to legal liabilities, regulatory fines, and reputational damage.

•   Compliance with standards helps government departments mitigate legal and financial risks by ensuring that they meet the requirements of relevant laws, regulations, and industry best practices, reducing the likelihood of compliance-related penalties and sanctions.

8.   Demonstrating Leadership and Accountability:

•   Compliance with standards and regulations demonstrates leadership and accountability on the part of government departments, showing a commitment to ethical conduct, responsible governance, and the protection of citizens' interests.

•   By adhering to established standards and best practices, government departments set an example for other organizations to follow, promoting a culture of compliance, integrity, and trustworthiness across the public sector.

Conclusion:

Compliance with regulatory requirements and adherence to established standards and best practices are essential for government departments to uphold the rule of law, protect sensitive information, and enhance public trust and confidence.

By ensuring compliance with legal and regulatory requirements, protecting sensitive information, strengthening cybersecurity and resilience, promoting efficiency and effectiveness, enhancing public trust and confidence, facilitating interoperability and collaboration, mitigating legal and financial risks, and demonstrating leadership and accountability, government departments can fulfil their mandate effectively and serve the interests of citizens in a transparent, accountable, and responsible manner.

Challenges and Opportunities in Implementing Regulatory Frameworks

Introduction:

Regulatory frameworks play a critical role in shaping the behaviour of organizations, ensuring compliance with legal requirements, and safeguarding the interests of stakeholders. However, implementing regulatory frameworks presents numerous challenges for both regulators and regulated entities, ranging from complexity and ambiguity to resource constraints and resistance to change.

This book examines the challenges and opportunities in implementing regulatory frameworks, highlighting key issues and strategies for overcoming obstacles and maximizing benefits.

1. Complexity and Ambiguity:

• Regulatory frameworks are often complex and subject to interpretation, posing challenges for regulated entities in understanding and complying with regulatory requirements.

• Ambiguity in regulatory language and lack of clarity in regulatory expectations can lead to confusion, inconsistent interpretation, and difficulty in achieving compliance.

2. Resource Constraints:

• Implementing regulatory frameworks requires significant resources, including financial, human, and technological resources, which may be limited for both regulators and regulated entities.

• Resource constraints can hinder the ability of regulators to enforce compliance and provide support and guidance to regulated entities, leading to gaps in regulatory oversight and enforcement.

3. Compliance Costs:

• Compliance with regulatory frameworks often entails costs for regulated entities, including investments in technology, personnel, training, and compliance monitoring and reporting.

• High compliance costs can be burdensome for small and medium-sized enterprises (SMEs) and startups, inhibiting innovation, competitiveness, and economic growth.

4. Regulatory Capture and Influence:

• Regulatory capture, where regulated entities exert undue influence over regulators, can undermine the effectiveness of regulatory frameworks and weaken regulatory oversight.

• Regulatory capture may result in lenient enforcement of regulations, regulatory capture, where regulated entities exert undue influence over regulators, can undermine the effectiveness of regulatory frameworks and weaken regulatory oversight.

5.   Resistance to Change:

•   Regulated entities may resist change and view regulatory compliance as burdensome, bureaucratic, and costly, particularly if they perceive regulatory requirements as unnecessary or excessive.

•   Resistance to change can impede efforts to implement regulatory frameworks effectively and achieve regulatory objectives, leading to non-compliance and increased regulatory risk.

6.   Enforcement Challenges:

•   Enforcing compliance with regulatory frameworks poses challenges for regulators, including identifying and investigating violations, gathering evidence, and imposing sanctions on non-compliant entities.

•   Limited resources, jurisdictional constraints, and legal complexities can hinder regulators' ability to enforce compliance effectively, leading to gaps in regulatory enforcement and impunity for non-compliant entities.

7.   Technological Advancements:

•   Technological advancements present both challenges and opportunities for implementing regulatory frameworks.

•   Emerging technologies, such as artificial intelligence (AI), blockchain, and the Internet of Things (IoT), can facilitate regulatory compliance through automation, data analytics, and real-time monitoring and reporting.

•   However, technological advancements also pose challenges for regulators in keeping pace with rapid technological change, understanding the implications of new technologies for regulatory oversight, and adapting regulatory frameworks to address emerging risks and challenges.

8.   Stakeholder Engagement and Collaboration:

•   Effective implementation of regulatory frameworks requires stakeholder engagement and collaboration between regulators, regulated entities, industry associations, consumer groups, and other relevant stakeholders.

• Stakeholder engagement promotes transparency, accountability, and trust in the regulatory process, facilitates the exchange of information and best practices, and enhances compliance with regulatory requirements.

Opportunities in Implementing Regulatory Frameworks:

• Despite the challenges, implementing regulatory frameworks presents opportunities for regulators and regulated entities to enhance transparency, accountability, and trust in the regulatory process, promote innovation and competitiveness, and protect the interests of stakeholders.

• Leveraging technology, data analytics, and automation can streamline regulatory processes, improve regulatory oversight, and enhance compliance with regulatory requirements.

• Enhancing stakeholder engagement, collaboration, and communication can foster a culture of compliance, promote dialogue and cooperation between regulators and regulated entities, and facilitate the development of effective and proportionate regulatory solutions.

• Investing in capacity building, training, and awareness-raising initiatives can enhance regulatory capacity, empower regulators and regulated entities to meet regulatory challenges, and build a culture of compliance and regulatory excellence.

Conclusion:

Implementing regulatory frameworks presents numerous challenges for regulators and regulated entities, including complexity, resource constraints, compliance costs, regulatory capture, resistance to change, enforcement challenges, and technological advancements.

However, these challenges also present opportunities for regulators and regulated entities to enhance transparency, accountability, and trust in the regulatory process, promote innovation and competitiveness, and protect the interests of stakeholders. By leveraging technology, enhancing stakeholder engagement, and investing in capacity building and awareness-raising initiatives, regulators and regulated entities can overcome regulatory challenges, achieve regulatory objectives, and realize the benefits of effective regulatory frameworks.

Chapter 7: International Cooperation and Partnerships

In today's interconnected and interdependent world, cyber threats transcend national boundaries, requiring collective action and collaboration among countries, international organizations, and other stakeholders to address common cybersecurity challenges effectively. International cooperation and partnerships play a crucial role in enhancing cybersecurity resilience, promoting information sharing, fostering capacity building, and combating cybercrime and cyber threats on a global scale.

This chapter explores the importance of international cooperation and partnerships in cybersecurity, highlighting key initiatives, challenges, and opportunities for collaboration in the international arena.

1.   Importance of International Cooperation in Cybersecurity:

•   Cyber threats are global in nature and do not respect national borders, requiring coordinated and collaborative efforts among countries to address effectively.

•   International cooperation in cybersecurity enables countries to share threat intelligence, best practices, and technical expertise, enhance cybersecurity capabilities, and respond collectively to cyber incidents and emerging threats.

2.   Key Initiatives and Platforms for International Cooperation:

•   Several international initiatives and platforms facilitate cooperation and collaboration in cybersecurity, including:

•   United Nations: The United Nations (UN) promotes international cooperation in cybersecurity through various initiatives, including the UN Group of Governmental Experts (GGE) on Developments in the

Field of Information and Telecommunications in the Context of International Security.

• International Telecommunication Union (ITU): The ITU works to enhance cybersecurity capacity building, promote cybersecurity awareness, and develop international cybersecurity standards and guidelines.

• INTERPOL: INTERPOL facilitates cooperation and information sharing among law enforcement agencies worldwide to combat cybercrime and cyber threats.

• Global Forum on Cyber Expertise (GFCE): The GFCE fosters international cooperation in cybersecurity capacity building through knowledge sharing, networking, and collaboration among governments, international organizations, and other stakeholders.

3. Challenges in International Cooperation:

• Despite the importance of international cooperation in cybersecurity, several challenges hinder effective collaboration among countries, including:

• Geopolitical tensions and diplomatic disputes can hamper trust and cooperation among countries, limiting information sharing and collaboration on cybersecurity issues.

• Legal and jurisdictional differences among countries complicate efforts to harmonize cybersecurity laws, regulations, and enforcement mechanisms, leading to gaps in international cooperation and coordination.

• Resource disparities between developed and developing countries can hinder efforts to build cybersecurity capacity and address cyber threats effectively, exacerbating global cybersecurity inequalities.

4. Opportunities for International Cooperation:

• Despite the challenges, international cooperation in cybersecurity presents significant opportunities for countries to enhance cybersecurity resilience, promote innovation, and strengthen global cybersecurity governance:

• Multilateral forums and initiatives provide platforms for countries to engage in dialogue, exchange best practices, and develop norms of responsible behaviour in cyberspace, fostering trust and confidence among nations.

• Public-private partnerships facilitate collaboration between governments, industry, academia, and civil society to address cybersecurity challenges collectively, leveraging diverse expertise, resources, and capabilities to enhance cyber resilience and combat cyber threats.

• Regional cooperation initiatives enable countries to pool resources, share threat intelligence, and coordinate responses to cyber incidents and emerging threats within specific geographical regions, fostering a sense of solidarity and cooperation among neighbouring countries.

5. Best Practices for International Cooperation:

• To maximize the benefits of international cooperation in cybersecurity, countries can adopt several best practices, including:

• Establishing formal mechanisms for bilateral and multilateral cooperation, such as information sharing agreements, mutual assistance treaties, and joint cybersecurity exercises, to facilitate collaboration and coordination among countries.

• Investing in capacity building and technical assistance programs to support developing countries in enhancing their cybersecurity capabilities, promoting cybersecurity awareness, and strengthening legal and regulatory frameworks.

• Promoting a culture of trust, transparency, and openness in international cooperation efforts, fostering confidence-building measures, and respecting the sovereignty and independence of participating countries.

Conclusion:

International cooperation and partnerships are essential for addressing the complex and evolving challenges of cybersecurity in today's interconnected world. By leveraging multilateral forums, regional initiatives, public-private partnerships, and best practices in international cooperation, countries can enhance cybersecurity resilience, promote information sharing, foster capacity building, and combat cybercrime and cyber threats on a global scale.

Despite the challenges, the opportunities for collaboration in cybersecurity are vast, and by working together, countries can strengthen global cybersecurity governance, promote stability and security in cyberspace, and safeguard the interests of individuals, organizations, and nations alike.

Importance of International Collaboration in Combatting Cyber Threats

In an increasingly interconnected and digitized world, cyber threats have become a significant concern for governments, businesses, and individuals alike. These threats do not respect national borders and often require coordinated efforts among countries to effectively address them.

International collaboration plays a crucial role in combatting cyber threats by facilitating information sharing, promoting best practices, enhancing cyber resilience, and fostering cooperation among nations.

This book explores the importance of international collaboration in combatting cyber threats, highlighting key benefits, challenges, and strategies for effective collaboration.

1.   Global Nature of Cyber Threats:

•   Cyber threats, such as malware, ransomware, phishing attacks, and distributed denial-of-service (DDoS) attacks, can originate from anywhere in the world and target entities across borders indiscriminately.

•   The interconnected nature of the internet and digital networks means that cyber-attacks can have far-reaching consequences, impacting multiple countries, industries, and critical infrastructure sectors simultaneously.

2. Need for Collective Response:

•   Given the global nature of cyber threats, no single country or organization can address them effectively in isolation. A collective response involving international collaboration is essential to combatting cyber threats comprehensively.

•   International collaboration enables countries to share threat intelligence, coordinate responses to cyber incidents, and develop joint strategies for mitigating cyber risks and vulnerabilities.

3. Benefits of International Collaboration:

•   International collaboration offers several key benefits in combatting cyber threats:

•   Enhanced Threat Intelligence Sharing: Collaborative efforts enable countries to share timely and actionable threat intelligence, enabling faster detection and response to cyber threats.

• Improved Cyber Resilience: By sharing best practices, expertise, and resources, countries can enhance their cyber resilience and better withstand cyber-attacks and disruptions.

• Coordinated Response to Cyber Incidents: International collaboration facilitates coordinated responses to cyber incidents, enabling affected countries to pool resources, coordinate investigations, and take collective action against cyber adversaries.

• Strengthened Legal and Regulatory Frameworks: Collaborative efforts help countries harmonize their legal and regulatory frameworks for cybercrime, enabling more effective prosecution of cyber criminals and greater deterrence against cyber-attacks.

• Capacity Building and Training: International collaboration supports capacity building and training initiatives, empowering countries to develop the skills and capabilities needed to address cyber threats effectively and build a cyber-resilient workforce.

4. Challenges in International Collaboration:

• Despite the benefits, international collaboration in combatting cyber threats faces several challenges:

• Legal and Jurisdictional Differences: Variations in legal frameworks and jurisdictional boundaries among countries can complicate efforts to coordinate responses to cyber incidents and enforce cybercrime laws internationally.

• Geopolitical Tensions: Political tensions and diplomatic disputes between countries can hinder cooperation and information sharing on cyber threats, leading to gaps in collective cyber defence.

• Resource Disparities: Resource disparities among countries, particularly between developed and developing nations, can limit the effectiveness of international collaboration efforts, hindering capacity building and information sharing initiatives.

• Trust and Information Sharing: Establishing trust and confidence among countries for sharing sensitive threat intelligence and cybersecurity information can be challenging, especially in the absence of clear protocols and frameworks for information sharing.

5. Strategies for Effective Collaboration:

•   To overcome challenges and maximize the benefits of international collaboration in combatting cyber threats, countries can adopt several strategies:

•   Establish Formal Mechanisms for Information Sharing: Countries can establish formal mechanisms, such as information sharing agreements, bilateral partnerships, and international organizations, to facilitate information sharing and collaboration on cyber threats.

•   Foster Trust and Confidence: Building trust and confidence among countries is crucial for effective collaboration. Countries can achieve this through transparency, reciprocity, and adherence to agreed-upon principles and norms for cybersecurity.

•   Strengthen Legal and Regulatory Frameworks: Harmonizing legal and regulatory frameworks for cybercrime and cybersecurity among countries can facilitate cross-border cooperation and streamline international law enforcement efforts.

• Promote Capacity Building and Training: Supporting capacity building and training initiatives, particularly in developing countries, can enhance cyber resilience and empower countries to address cyber threats effectively.

Conclusion:

International collaboration is essential for combatting cyber threats in today's interconnected world. By sharing threat intelligence, coordinating responses to cyber incidents, and fostering cooperation among nations, countries can enhance their cyber resilience and better protect their citizens, businesses, and critical infrastructure from cyber-attacks.

Despite the challenges, the benefits of international collaboration in combatting cyber threats are substantial, and by working together, countries can strengthen global cybersecurity governance, promote stability and security in cyberspace, and safeguard the digital economy and society for future generations.

Initiatives and Platforms for Information Sharing and Mutual Assistance

In the face of escalating cyber threats and attacks, collaboration and information sharing among stakeholders have become essential components of effective cybersecurity strategies. Governments, businesses, and other organizations need to exchange threat intelligence, best practices, and resources to bolster their defences and respond swiftly to cyber incidents.

This book explores various initiatives and platforms established for information sharing and mutual assistance in cybersecurity, highlighting their significance, benefits, challenges, and future prospects.

1.   Importance of Information Sharing and Mutual Assistance:

•   Cyber threats are dynamic and constantly evolving, making it challenging for organizations to keep pace with the latest threats and vulnerabilities on their own.

•   Information sharing and mutual assistance enable organizations to leverage collective knowledge, resources, and expertise to identify and mitigate cyber risks effectively.

2.   Government-led Initiatives:

•   Governments play a central role in fostering information sharing and mutual assistance in cybersecurity through various initiatives and programs:

•   National Computer Emergency Response Teams (CERTs): Many countries have established CERTs to coordinate responses to cyber incidents, disseminate threat intelligence, and provide technical assistance to organizations.

- Information Sharing and Analysis Centres (ISACs): ISACs bring together stakeholders from specific industries or sectors to share threat intelligence, collaborate on cybersecurity issues, and develop best practices for cyber defence.

- Public-Private Partnerships: Governments collaborate with the private sector and academia to facilitate information sharing, conduct joint cybersecurity exercises, and enhance cyber resilience across critical infrastructure sectors.

3. International Organizations and Initiatives:

- International organizations play a vital role in promoting information sharing and mutual assistance in cybersecurity on a global scale:

- Forum of Incident Response and Security Teams (FIRST): FIRST is a global organization that coordinates responses to cyber incidents, facilitates information sharing among member teams, and promotes collaboration on cybersecurity issues.

• Global Cyber Alliance (GCA): GCA brings together public and private sector partners to address cyber risks and promote cybersecurity best practices, particularly among small and medium-sized enterprises (SMEs) and underserved communities.

• Cyber Threat Intelligence Sharing Platforms: International organizations develop and maintain platforms for sharing threat intelligence, such as the Cyber Threat Alliance (CTA) and the Cyber Information Sharing and Collaboration Program (CISCP), to enable timely and actionable information sharing among members.

4. Private Sector Initiatives:

• The private sector plays a critical role in fostering information sharing and mutual assistance in cybersecurity through industry-led initiatives and platforms:

• Information Sharing and Analysis Centres (ISACs): Private sector ISACs, such as the Financial Services ISAC (FS-ISAC) and the Healthcare ISAC (H-ISAC), facilitate information sharing and collaboration among organizations within specific industries or sectors.

• Sector-specific Collaborative Platforms: Companies within the same industry or sector collaborate through sector-specific collaborative platforms, such as the Retail Cyber Intelligence Sharing Centre (R-CISC) and the Automotive Information Sharing and Analysis Centre (Auto-ISAC), to share threat intelligence and best practices for cyber defence.

5.   Challenges in Information Sharing and Mutual Assistance:

• Despite the benefits, information sharing and mutual assistance in cybersecurity face several challenges:

• Legal and Regulatory Constraints: Concerns about privacy, data protection, and liability can impede information sharing and collaboration among organizations, particularly across borders.

• Trust and Confidentiality: Establishing trust and confidentiality among participants is essential for effective information sharing but concerns about data misuse and attribution can hinder collaboration.

• Technical Compatibility: Differences in technical platforms, data formats, and information sharing protocols among organizations can complicate efforts to exchange threat intelligence and collaborate effectively.

6. Strategies for Overcoming Challenges:

• To overcome challenges and maximize the benefits of information sharing and mutual assistance in cybersecurity, organizations can adopt several strategies:

• Establish Clear Guidelines and Protocols: Developing clear guidelines and protocols for information sharing, including data handling procedures, confidentiality agreements, and incident reporting mechanisms, can enhance trust and facilitate collaboration.

• Foster Collaboration and Trust: Building relationships and fostering collaboration among participants through regular communication, joint exercises, and shared experiences can strengthen trust and facilitate effective information sharing.

• Invest in Technical Solutions: Investing in interoperable technical solutions and platforms for sharing threat intelligence, such as standardized data formats and secure communication channels, can streamline information sharing and enhance collaboration.

Conclusion:

Information sharing and mutual assistance are essential pillars of effective cybersecurity strategies, enabling organizations to identify and mitigate cyber risks more effectively. Through government-led initiatives, international cooperation, and private sector collaboration, stakeholders can leverage collective knowledge, resources, and expertise to enhance cyber resilience and respond swiftly to cyber threats and incidents.

Despite the challenges, continued investment in information sharing platforms, collaboration frameworks, and capacity building initiatives will be crucial for addressing evolving cyber threats and ensuring the security and stability of cyberspace for all stakeholders.

Case Studies Highlighting Successful Collaborative Efforts in Cybersecurity

Collaborative efforts among stakeholders are essential for addressing the complex and evolving landscape of cyber threats effectively. Successful case studies demonstrate how organizations, governments, and international bodies have collaborated to enhance cybersecurity resilience, share threat intelligence, and respond to cyber incidents.

This book presents case studies highlighting successful collaborative efforts in cybersecurity, examining key initiatives, strategies, and outcomes that have contributed to improved cybersecurity outcomes.

1. The Cyber Threat Alliance (CTA):

• The Cyber Threat Alliance (CTA) is a collaborative effort among cybersecurity vendors and researchers aimed at sharing threat intelligence and coordinating responses to cyber threats.

• Members of the CTA collaborate to collect, analyse, and disseminate threat intelligence on emerging cyber threats, such as malware, ransomware, and phishing attacks.

• By sharing timely and actionable threat intelligence, CTA members can better protect their customers, identify emerging threats, and disrupt cybercriminal activities.

• The CTA's collaborative approach has led to the identification and mitigation of numerous cyber threats, enhancing cybersecurity resilience across the industry.

2.   The Financial Services Information Sharing and Analysis centre (FS-ISAC):

•   The Financial Services Information Sharing and Analysis centre (FS-ISAC) is a sector-specific collaborative platform for sharing threat intelligence and best practices among financial institutions.

•   FS-ISAC members collaborate to share information on cyber threats targeting the financial sector, including fraud, data breaches, and cyber-attacks.

•   Through the FS-ISAC, financial institutions can better understand emerging threats, improve their cyber defences, and coordinate responses to cyber incidents.

•   The FS-ISAC's collaborative approach has helped financial institutions detect and mitigate cyber threats more effectively, reducing the risk of financial losses and reputational damage.

3. The National Cybersecurity centre of Excellence (NCCoE):

• The National Cybersecurity Center of Excellence (NCCoE) is a collaborative initiative between the National Institute of Standards and Technology (NIST), industry partners, and academia aimed at addressing cybersecurity challenges through practical solutions.

• The NCCoE collaborates with stakeholders to develop reference architectures, standards-based solutions, and best practices for securing various sectors, including healthcare, energy, and finance.

• By leveraging expertise from industry and academia, the NCCoE develops cybersecurity solutions that address real-world challenges, enhance cybersecurity resilience, and promote innovation.

• The NCCoE's collaborative approach has led to the development of cybersecurity solutions that have been adopted by organizations across sectors, improving their cybersecurity posture and reducing risk.

4.   The Global Cyber Alliance (GCA):

• The Global Cyber Alliance (GCA) is an international nonprofit organization that collaborates with partners from the public and private sectors to combat cyber threats and improve cybersecurity resilience.

• GCA focuses on developing practical solutions, promoting best practices, and raising awareness to address cyber risks and vulnerabilities.

• Through initiatives such as the Quad9 DNS service and the Cybersecurity Toolkit for Small Business, GCA provides tools and resources to help organizations enhance their cybersecurity defenses.

• GCA's collaborative approach has empowered organizations of all sizes to improve their cybersecurity resilience, protect against cyber threats, and mitigate risks effectively.

5.   The Forum of Incident Response and Security Teams (FIRST):

• The Forum of Incident Response and Security Teams (FIRST) is a global organization that brings together incident response teams from around the world to collaborate on cybersecurity incidents and share best practices.

• FIRST members collaborate to share incident data, coordinate responses to cyber incidents, and develop best practices for incident response and security.

• By sharing information and expertise, FIRST members can respond more effectively to cyber incidents, minimize the impact of cyber-attacks, and strengthen their cybersecurity defences.

• FIRST's collaborative approach has facilitated rapid and coordinated responses to cyber incidents, helping organizations recover quickly and minimize damage.

Conclusion:

Successful case studies demonstrate the value of collaborative efforts in cybersecurity, enabling stakeholders to share threat intelligence, coordinate responses to cyber threats, and develop practical solutions to enhance cybersecurity resilience.

Initiatives such as the Cyber Threat Alliance, Financial Services Information Sharing and Analysis Center, National Cybersecurity Center of Excellence, Global Cyber Alliance, and Forum of Incident Response and Security Teams exemplify the benefits of collaboration in addressing complex cybersecurity challenges. By working together, organizations, governments, and international bodies can strengthen cybersecurity defences, mitigate cyber risks, and protect against emerging threats in an increasingly interconnected and digital world.

Chapter 8: Cybersecurity Governance and Leadership

In the digital age, where information is exchanged at lightning speed and cyber threats loom large, effective cybersecurity governance and leadership are paramount. Chapter 8 delves into the intricate landscape of cybersecurity governance, emphasizing the critical role of leadership in safeguarding organizational assets against evolving threats. From establishing robust frameworks to fostering a culture of security awareness, this chapter navigates the multifaceted terrain of cyber governance with an eye towards resilience and adaptability.

At the heart of cybersecurity governance lies the need for clear policies and procedures that dictate how organizations manage their cyber risks. This involves defining roles and responsibilities, establishing accountability structures, and aligning cybersecurity objectives with overarching business goals. Through frameworks such as NIST Cybersecurity Framework and ISO 27001, organizations can systematically assess their cybersecurity posture and implement controls to mitigate risks effectively.

Leadership plays a pivotal role in driving cybersecurity initiatives from the top down. C-suite executives and board members must champion cybersecurity as a strategic priority and allocate sufficient resources to support it. By fostering a culture of cybersecurity awareness and accountability, leaders can empower employees to become active participants in safeguarding the organization's digital assets.

Effective cybersecurity governance requires collaboration across departments and stakeholders. IT teams, legal counsel, compliance officers, and risk management professionals must work in tandem to identify, assess, and mitigate cyber risks comprehensively. By fostering cross-functional collaboration and communication, organizations can ensure a holistic approach to cybersecurity governance that addresses both technical vulnerabilities and regulatory requirements.

One of the key challenges in cybersecurity governance is staying ahead of emerging threats and technologies. Leaders must remain vigilant and adaptable, continuously monitoring the threat landscape and evaluating new cybersecurity solutions. By investing in research and development, organizations can proactively identify and address potential vulnerabilities before they are exploited by malicious actors.

In addition to proactive measures, effective cybersecurity governance also requires a robust incident response plan. Leaders must establish clear protocols for detecting, responding to, and recovering from cyber incidents. This involves conducting regular tabletop exercises and simulations to test the organization's readiness to handle various cyber threats.

Furthermore, cybersecurity governance extends beyond the boundaries of individual organizations. In an interconnected ecosystem, collaboration with industry peers, government agencies, and international partners is essential to combating cyber threats effectively. Leaders must engage in information sharing and collective defence initiatives to strengthen cybersecurity resilience at both the organizational and national levels.

Ethical considerations also play a crucial role in cybersecurity governance and leadership. Leaders must uphold principles of transparency, integrity, and privacy in their cybersecurity practices. This involves respecting user consent, protecting sensitive data, and adhering to ethical guidelines in the development and deployment of cybersecurity technologies.

Moreover, diversity and inclusivity are essential for fostering innovation and resilience in cybersecurity governance. By promoting diversity in thought and experience, organizations can bring fresh perspectives to cybersecurity challenges and develop more robust solutions. Leaders must prioritize diversity and inclusion initiatives to ensure that cybersecurity teams reflect the diverse backgrounds and perspectives of the communities they serve.

Ultimately, effective cybersecurity governance and leadership require a proactive, collaborative, and ethical approach to managing cyber risks. By championing cybersecurity as a strategic imperative, fostering a culture of security awareness, and embracing diversity and inclusivity, leaders can strengthen their organizations' resilience against evolving cyber threats. In a rapidly changing digital landscape, the ability to adapt and innovate is key to staying one step ahead of cyber adversaries and safeguarding the integrity of critical systems and data.

The Role of Government Leaders in Championing Cybersecurity Initiatives

In an increasingly digital world where cyber threats pose significant risks to national security, economic stability, and individual privacy, the role of government leaders in championing cybersecurity initiatives is paramount. From setting policies and regulations to coordinating response efforts and fostering international cooperation, government leaders play a central role in safeguarding their nations' digital infrastructure and promoting cybersecurity resilience. This book explores the multifaceted responsibilities of government leaders in addressing cyber threats and advancing cybersecurity initiatives to protect their citizens and critical assets.

At the forefront of government leadership in cybersecurity is the formulation of policies and regulations that establish the framework for cybersecurity governance and enforcement. Government leaders must work closely with policymakers, regulatory agencies, and industry stakeholders to develop legislation and regulatory frameworks that address emerging cyber threats, promote best practices, and ensure compliance across sectors. By establishing clear standards and guidelines for cybersecurity, government leaders can create a conducive environment for organizations to prioritize cybersecurity investments and adopt proactive measures to mitigate risks.

In addition to policy development, government leaders are responsible for coordinating national cybersecurity strategies and response efforts. This involves collaboration across government agencies, law enforcement, intelligence agencies, and the private sector to identify threats, share information, and coordinate response actions effectively. Government leaders must establish mechanisms for real-time threat intelligence sharing, incident response coordination, and crisis management to enhance the nation's ability to detect, prevent, and respond to cyber-attacks promptly.

Moreover, government leaders play a crucial role in fostering a culture of cybersecurity awareness and education among citizens, businesses, and other stakeholders. By investing in public awareness campaigns, cybersecurity training programs, and educational initiatives, government leaders can empower individuals and organizations to recognize cyber risks, adopt secure practices, and take proactive measures to protect themselves from cyber threats. Promoting a cybersecurity-aware culture is essential for building resilience at the grassroots level and reducing the likelihood of successful cyber-attacks.

Furthermore, government leaders must engage in international cooperation and diplomacy to address transnational cyber threats effectively. Cyber-attacks often originate from foreign adversaries or criminal organizations operating across borders, making international collaboration essential for mitigating cyber risks and holding malicious actors accountable. Government leaders must work with their counterparts in other countries to establish norms of responsible behaviour in cyberspace, strengthen international cybersecurity partnerships, and coordinate efforts to combat cybercrime and cyber terrorism.

In addition to addressing external threats, government leaders must also prioritize cybersecurity resilience within their own organizations and critical infrastructure sectors. This involves investing in robust cybersecurity capabilities, conducting regular risk assessments, and implementing security controls to protect government networks, systems, and data from cyber attacks. Government leaders must lead by example by adhering to cybersecurity best practices, promoting transparency, and holding government agencies accountable for maintaining cybersecurity hygiene.

Furthermore, government leaders must support research and development initiatives to drive innovation in cybersecurity technology and solutions. By investing in cutting-edge research, fostering collaboration between academia, industry, and government, and incentivizing cybersecurity innovation, government leaders can advance the state of the art in cybersecurity and stay ahead of evolving cyber threats. Supporting cybersecurity innovation is essential for maintaining technological leadership, enhancing national security, and driving economic growth in the digital age.

In conclusion, the role of government leaders in championing cybersecurity initiatives is multifaceted and essential for protecting national security, promoting economic prosperity, and safeguarding individual privacy. From policy development and coordination of national cybersecurity strategies to fostering a culture of cybersecurity awareness and promoting international cooperation, government leaders have a critical responsibility to ensure that their nations are prepared to address the complex challenges of cyberspace effectively. By prioritizing cybersecurity and investing in proactive measures to mitigate cyber risks, government leaders can build resilience, enhance trust, and ensure the continued prosperity and security of their nations in an increasingly interconnected world.

Building Cybersecurity Awareness and Culture Across Government Departments

In today's digital age, where cyber threats continue to evolve in complexity and sophistication, building cybersecurity awareness and fostering a culture of security across government departments are imperative. Government agencies are entrusted with sensitive information, critical infrastructure, and essential services, making them prime targets for cyber-attacks. Therefore, it is essential to equip employees with the knowledge, skills, and mindset necessary to recognize and mitigate cyber risks effectively. This book explores the strategies and best practices for building cybersecurity awareness and culture across government departments to enhance resilience and protect against cyber threats.

1.   Education and Training Programs: One of the most effective ways to promote cybersecurity awareness is through comprehensive education and training programs. Government departments should develop tailored training modules that cover topics such as

identifying phishing attempts, practicing safe browsing habits, recognizing malware, and handling sensitive information securely. These programs should be mandatory for all employees and regularly updated to reflect emerging threats and best practices.

2.   Simulations and Exercises: Conducting simulated cyber-attack exercises can help government employees understand the potential impact of cyber threats and the importance of adhering to cybersecurity protocols. These exercises can simulate real-world scenarios, such as ransomware attacks or data breaches, and allow employees to practice their response procedures in a controlled environment. By experiencing firsthand the consequences of cyber-attacks, employees are more likely to take cybersecurity seriously and remain vigilant in their day-to-day activities.

3.   Leadership Support and Communication: Leadership support is essential for fostering a culture of cybersecurity within government departments. Senior leaders should actively promote cybersecurity awareness initiatives, communicate the importance of cybersecurity to employees, and lead by example in

adhering to security protocols. Regular communication from leadership about cybersecurity policies, procedures, and updates can help reinforce their importance and encourage employee compliance.

4.   Tailored Messaging and Outreach: Government departments should tailor their cybersecurity awareness messaging to resonate with their specific audience. Different departments may have varying levels of technical expertise and understanding of cybersecurity risks, so it's essential to communicate in a way that is accessible and relevant to all employees. Utilizing multiple communication channels, such as email, intranet portals, posters, and staff meetings, can help ensure that cybersecurity messages reach employees effectively.

5.   Promoting a Positive Security Culture: Building a positive security culture involves creating an environment where cybersecurity is seen as everyone's responsibility, not just the IT department's. Government departments should encourage employees to report security incidents promptly, ask questions about cybersecurity practices, and actively participate in

ongoing training and awareness efforts. Recognizing and rewarding employees who demonstrate exemplary cybersecurity behaviour can help reinforce desired attitudes and behaviours.

6.   Partnerships and Collaboration: Collaboration between government departments, industry partners, and other stakeholders can enhance cybersecurity awareness and culture across the broader ecosystem. Government agencies can leverage partnerships with industry associations, academic institutions, and cybersecurity experts to access resources, share best practices, and stay informed about emerging threats. By working together, stakeholders can collectively strengthen their cybersecurity posture and respond more effectively to cyber threats.

7.   Regular Assessments and Feedback: Ongoing evaluation and feedback mechanisms are essential for measuring the effectiveness of cybersecurity awareness initiatives and identifying areas for improvement. Government departments should conduct regular assessments, such as surveys or quizzes, to gauge employees' understanding of cybersecurity concepts

and identify any gaps in knowledge or awareness. Feedback from employees can help inform future training programs and awareness campaigns, ensuring that they remain relevant and impactful.

8.   Continuous Learning and Adaptation: Cyber threats are constantly evolving, so cybersecurity awareness efforts must adapt accordingly. Government departments should stay abreast of the latest cybersecurity trends, technologies, and best practices and incorporate this knowledge into their awareness initiatives. Continuous learning opportunities, such as webinars, conferences, and professional development courses, can help employees stay informed about emerging threats and enhance their cybersecurity skills over time.

In conclusion, building cybersecurity awareness and fostering a culture of security across government departments is essential for protecting sensitive information, critical infrastructure, and essential services from cyber threats. By implementing comprehensive education and training programs, conducting simulated exercises, garnering leadership support, tailoring messaging, promoting a positive security culture, fostering partnerships, soliciting feedback, and embracing continuous learning, government agencies can empower employees to recognize and mitigate cyber risks effectively. By prioritizing cybersecurity awareness and culture, government departments can enhance resilience, minimize vulnerabilities, and safeguard the nation's digital assets in an increasingly interconnected and complex threat landscape.

Encouraging Innovation and Adaptation in the Face of Evolving Threats

In today's rapidly evolving cybersecurity landscape, where cyber threats are becoming increasingly sophisticated and pervasive, encouraging innovation and adaptation is crucial for staying ahead of adversaries and protecting critical assets. The traditional approach of relying solely on static defences and reactive measures is no longer sufficient in the face of dynamic and constantly evolving cyber threats. Instead, organizations must foster a culture of innovation and adaptation that empowers them to anticipate, respond to, and mitigate emerging cyber risks effectively. This book explores the importance of encouraging innovation and adaptation in cybersecurity and outlines strategies for organizations to cultivate a culture of resilience in the face of evolving threats.

1.   Anticipating Emerging Threats: Encouraging innovation in cybersecurity begins with the ability to anticipate emerging threats before they materialize. Organizations must invest in threat intelligence capabilities and proactive threat hunting techniques to identify potential vulnerabilities and emerging attack vectors. By staying ahead of the curve and anticipating cyber threats before they become widespread, organizations can develop pre-emptive strategies to mitigate risks and minimize potential damage.

2.   Embracing Emerging Technologies: Innovation in cybersecurity often involves leveraging emerging technologies to enhance defence capabilities and improve threat detection and response. Technologies such as artificial intelligence (AI), machine learning (ML), behavioural analytics, and automation can help organizations detect anomalies, identify patterns of malicious behaviour, and respond to threats in real time.

By embracing emerging technologies, organizations can strengthen their cybersecurity posture and adapt to evolving threats more effectively.

3.   Promoting Collaboration and Information Sharing: Collaboration and information sharing among industry peers, government agencies, and cybersecurity professionals are essential for staying abreast of emerging threats and best practices. Organizations should participate in information sharing initiatives, such as threat intelligence sharing platforms and industry-specific information sharing and analysis centers (ISACs), to exchange actionable intelligence and insights about cyber threats. By pooling resources and expertise, organizations can enhance their collective resilience and adaptability to evolving threats.

4.   Encouraging a Culture of Experimentation: Innovation thrives in environments where experimentation is encouraged and failure is viewed as an opportunity for learning and improvement. Organizations should create a culture that values creativity, curiosity, and risk-taking, where employees feel empowered to explore new ideas and approaches

to cybersecurity. By fostering a culture of experimentation, organizations can identify innovative solutions to complex cybersecurity challenges and adapt their strategies in response to evolving threats.

5.   Investing in Research and Development: Continuous investment in research and development (R&D) is essential for driving innovation in cybersecurity. Organizations should allocate resources to fund R&D initiatives that explore emerging technologies, novel defence mechanisms, and new approaches to cybersecurity. By investing in R&D, organizations can develop cutting-edge solutions that address the evolving threat landscape and provide a competitive advantage in the fight against cyber threats.

6.   Adopting Agile and Adaptive Security Frameworks: Traditional approaches to cybersecurity often rely on rigid, one-size-fits-all security frameworks that may not adequately address the dynamic nature of cyber threats. Agile and adaptive security frameworks, such as the NIST Cybersecurity Framework and the MITRE ATT&CK framework, provide organizations with flexible and adaptable frameworks for managing cyber risks.

These frameworks emphasize continuous monitoring, rapid detection and response, and iterative improvement, enabling organizations to adapt their security posture in real time based on evolving threats and changing business needs.

7.   Promoting Cross-Functional Collaboration: Cybersecurity is not solely the responsibility of the IT department but requires collaboration across all business functions. Organizations should promote cross-functional collaboration between IT, security, legal, compliance, risk management, and other relevant departments to ensure a holistic and coordinated approach to cybersecurity. By breaking down silos and fostering collaboration, organizations can leverage the collective expertise and resources of diverse teams to address cybersecurity challenges more effectively.

8.   Encouraging Diversity and Inclusion: Diversity and inclusion are essential for fostering innovation and creativity in cybersecurity. Organizations should prioritize diversity and inclusion initiatives to ensure that cybersecurity teams reflect a wide range of perspectives, backgrounds, and experiences. By

embracing diversity and inclusion, organizations can tap into a diverse talent pool, foster a culture of innovation, and develop more resilient cybersecurity strategies that are better equipped to adapt to evolving threats.

In conclusion, encouraging innovation and adaptation is essential for organizations to stay ahead of evolving cyber threats and protect critical assets effectively. By anticipating emerging threats, embracing emerging technologies, promoting collaboration and information sharing, encouraging a culture of experimentation, investing in R&D, adopting agile and adaptive security frameworks, promoting cross-functional collaboration, and encouraging diversity and inclusion, organizations can cultivate a culture of resilience that enables them to adapt to the ever-changing cybersecurity landscape. By fostering a culture of innovation and adaptation, organizations can strengthen their cybersecurity posture, mitigate risks, and protect against evolving threats in an increasingly complex and interconnected digital world.

Chapter 9: Emerging Technologies and Future Trends

In the rapidly evolving landscape of cybersecurity, staying abreast of emerging technologies and future trends is essential for organizations to adapt and effectively mitigate cyber threats. Chapter 9 delves into the exciting realm of emerging technologies and future trends in cybersecurity, exploring innovative solutions and strategies that promise to shape the future of cyber defence. From artificial intelligence and quantum computing to the Internet of Things and blockchain, this chapter examines the potential impact of these technologies on cybersecurity and offers insights into how organizations can leverage them to enhance their defences and stay ahead of cyber adversaries.

1. Artificial Intelligence and Machine Learning: Artificial intelligence (AI) and machine learning (ML) are revolutionizing cybersecurity by enabling organizations to automate threat detection, analyse vast amounts of data, and identify patterns of malicious behaviour in real

time. AI-powered security solutions can augment human capabilities, improving the speed and accuracy of threat detection and response. From anomaly detection and predictive analytics to user behaviour analysis and threat hunting, AI and ML have the potential to transform every aspect of cybersecurity, enabling organizations to proactively defend against evolving threats.

2.   Quantum Computing: Quantum computing represents a paradigm shift in computing power, with the potential to break traditional cryptographic algorithms and render current encryption methods obsolete. While quantum computing offers tremendous opportunities for scientific breakthroughs and technological innovation, it also poses significant challenges for cybersecurity. Organizations must prepare for the post-quantum era by developing quantum-resistant encryption algorithms and deploying quantum-safe cryptographic solutions to protect sensitive data from future quantum threats.

3.   Internet of Things (IoT): The proliferation of Internet-connected devices in the Internet of Things (IoT) presents both opportunities and challenges for

cybersecurity. IoT devices often lack robust security features, making them vulnerable to cyber-attacks and exploitation. Organizations must implement security measures to secure IoT devices, such as strong authentication, encryption, and regular firmware updates. Additionally, leveraging technologies like network segmentation and IoT security platforms can help organizations detect and mitigate IoT-related threats effectively.

4.   Blockchain Technology: Blockchain technology offers a decentralized and immutable ledger that can enhance the security and integrity of data transactions. In cybersecurity, blockchain has applications in areas such as secure authentication, identity management, supply chain security, and secure data sharing. By leveraging blockchain technology, organizations can establish trust, transparency, and accountability in their digital transactions, reducing the risk of fraud, tampering, and data manipulation.

5.   Cloud Security: As organizations increasingly migrate their operations to the cloud, ensuring the security of cloud environments becomes paramount.

Cloud security solutions, such as cloud access security brokers (CASBs), cloud security posture management (CSPM) tools, and cloud workload protection platforms (CWPPs), help organizations secure their cloud assets and data from unauthorized access, data breaches, and other cloud-related threats. Additionally, implementing cloud-native security controls and best practices, such as encryption, identity and access management (IAM), and continuous monitoring, can enhance the security of cloud environments and mitigate risks effectively.

6.   Zero Trust Security: Zero Trust security is an emerging security model that challenges the traditional perimeter-based approach to cybersecurity. Instead of trusting users and devices based on their location within the network perimeter, Zero Trust security assumes that all users, devices, and applications are untrusted and verifies their identity and access rights continuously. By implementing Zero Trust principles, such as least privilege access, micro-segmentation, and continuous authentication, organizations can reduce the risk of insider threats, lateral movement, and unauthorized access, enhancing their overall security posture.

7. Biometric Authentication: Biometric authentication offers a secure and convenient method of verifying users' identities based on unique biological traits, such as fingerprints, iris patterns, and facial recognition. By replacing traditional password-based authentication methods, biometric authentication can mitigate the risk of credential theft, phishing, and other common cyber-attacks. However, organizations must address privacy concerns and ensure the security of biometric data by implementing robust encryption and authentication protocols.

8. Cybersecurity Automation and Orchestration: Cybersecurity automation and orchestration solutions enable organizations to automate routine security tasks, streamline incident response workflows, and improve the efficiency of security operations. By integrating security tools and technologies through automation and orchestration platforms, organizations can accelerate threat detection and response, reduce manual errors, and free up security personnel to focus on strategic initiatives. Additionally, leveraging artificial intelligence and machine learning algorithms can further enhance

the effectiveness of cybersecurity automation and orchestration solutions.

In conclusion, Chapter 9 explores the exciting frontier of emerging technologies and future trends in cybersecurity, offering insights into innovative solutions and strategies that organizations can leverage to enhance their defences and stay ahead of cyber adversaries. From artificial intelligence and quantum computing to the Internet of Things and blockchain, these technologies have the potential to transform every aspect of cybersecurity, enabling organizations to adapt and thrive in an increasingly complex and dynamic threat landscape. By embracing emerging technologies and staying abreast of future trends, organizations can enhance their resilience, agility, and effectiveness in defending against evolving cyber threats.

The Impact of Emerging Technologies on Government Cybersecurity

Emerging technologies are revolutionizing the landscape of government cybersecurity, presenting both opportunities and challenges for protecting sensitive information, critical infrastructure, and essential services. From artificial intelligence and machine learning to quantum computing and blockchain, these technologies have the potential to transform how governments defend against cyber threats, enhance their resilience, and adapt to the evolving threat landscape. This book explores the impact of emerging technologies on government cybersecurity and outlines strategies for leveraging these technologies to strengthen cybersecurity defences effectively.

1.   Artificial Intelligence and Machine Learning: Artificial intelligence (AI) and machine learning (ML) are reshaping government cybersecurity by enabling organizations to automate threat detection, analyse vast amounts of data, and identify patterns of malicious behaviour in real time. Government agencies can leverage AI-powered security solutions to augment human capabilities, improve the speed and accuracy of threat detection and response, and enhance overall cybersecurity posture. By deploying AI and ML algorithms across their networks and systems,

government organizations can proactively identify and mitigate cyber threats before they escalate, thereby strengthening their resilience against cyber-attacks.

2. Quantum Computing: Quantum computing represents a paradigm shift in computing power, with the potential to break traditional cryptographic algorithms and render current encryption methods obsolete. While quantum computing offers tremendous opportunities for scientific breakthroughs and technological innovation, it also poses significant challenges for government cybersecurity. Government agencies must prepare for the post-quantum era by developing quantum-resistant encryption algorithms, deploying quantum-safe cryptographic solutions, and investing in research and development (R&D) initiatives to mitigate the potential impact of quantum threats on national security and critical infrastructure.

3. Internet of Things (IoT): The proliferation of Internet-connected devices in the Internet of Things (IoT) presents both opportunities and challenges for government cybersecurity. IoT devices, such as sensors, cameras, and smart appliances, often lack

robust security features, making them vulnerable to cyber-attacks and exploitation. Government agencies must implement security measures to secure IoT devices, such as strong authentication, encryption, and regular firmware updates. Additionally, leveraging technologies like network segmentation and IoT security platforms can help government organizations detect and mitigate IoT-related threats effectively, thereby safeguarding critical infrastructure and sensitive data from cyber-attacks.

4.   Blockchain Technology: Blockchain technology offers a decentralized and immutable ledger that can enhance the security and integrity of government transactions and data exchanges. In government cybersecurity, blockchain has applications in areas such as secure authentication, identity management, supply chain security, and secure data sharing. By leveraging blockchain technology, government agencies can establish trust, transparency, and accountability in their digital transactions, reduce the risk of fraud, tampering, and data manipulation, and enhance the resilience of government systems and networks against cyber-attacks.

5.   Cloud Security: As government agencies increasingly migrate their operations to the cloud, ensuring the security of cloud environments becomes paramount. Cloud security solutions, such as cloud access security brokers (CASBs), cloud security posture management (CSPM) tools, and cloud workload protection platforms (CWPPs), help government organizations secure their cloud assets and data from unauthorized access, data breaches, and other cloud-related threats. Additionally, implementing cloud-native security controls and best practices, such as encryption, identity and access management (IAM), and continuous monitoring, can enhance the security of government cloud environments and mitigate risks effectively.

6.   Zero Trust Security: Zero Trust security is an emerging security model that challenges the traditional perimeter-based approach to cybersecurity. Instead of trusting users and devices based on their location within the network perimeter, Zero Trust security assumes that all users, devices, and applications are untrusted and verifies their identity and access rights continuously. Government agencies can adopt Zero Trust principles,

such as least privilege access, micro-segmentation, and continuous authentication, to reduce the risk of insider threats, lateral movement, and unauthorized access, thereby enhancing the overall security posture of government systems and networks.

7. Biometric Authentication: Biometric authentication offers a secure and convenient method of verifying individuals' identities based on unique biological traits, such as fingerprints, iris patterns, and facial recognition. Government agencies can leverage biometric authentication to enhance the security of access control systems, secure sensitive facilities and information, and prevent unauthorized access to government networks and systems. However, government organizations must address privacy concerns and ensure the security of biometric data by implementing robust encryption and authentication protocols, complying with relevant regulations and guidelines, and adopting best practices for biometric data management and protection.

8. Cybersecurity Automation and Orchestration: Cybersecurity automation and orchestration solutions enable government agencies to automate routine

security tasks, streamline incident response workflows, and improve the efficiency of security operations. By integrating security tools and technologies through automation and orchestration platforms, government organizations can accelerate threat detection and response, reduce manual errors, and free up security personnel to focus on strategic initiatives. Additionally, leveraging artificial intelligence and machine learning algorithms can further enhance the effectiveness of cybersecurity automation and orchestration solutions, enabling government agencies to adapt to the evolving threat landscape and mitigate cyber risks effectively.

In conclusion, emerging technologies have the potential to transform government cybersecurity by enhancing threat detection and response capabilities, improving resilience against cyber-attacks, and enabling government organizations to adapt to the evolving threat landscape effectively. By leveraging technologies such as artificial intelligence, quantum computing, blockchain, IoT security, cloud security, Zero Trust security, biometric authentication, and cybersecurity automation and orchestration, government agencies can strengthen their cybersecurity defences, safeguard critical infrastructure and sensitive data, and uphold national security and public trust in an increasingly digital and interconnected world.

Opportunities and Challenges Presented by Artificial Intelligence, Internet of Things, and Blockchain

Artificial intelligence (AI), Internet of Things (IoT), and blockchain are three transformative technologies that are reshaping industries, revolutionizing processes, and presenting both opportunities and challenges in various domains. In the realm of cybersecurity, these technologies offer immense potential for enhancing threat detection, improving operational efficiency, and ensuring data integrity.

However, they also introduce new risks and complexities that must be addressed to harness their full potential effectively. This book explores the opportunities and challenges presented by AI, IoT, and blockchain in the context of cybersecurity and outlines strategies for organizations to navigate these technologies securely and effectively.

1.   Artificial Intelligence (AI):
Opportunities:

•   Enhanced Threat Detection: AI-powered cybersecurity solutions can analyse vast amounts of data in real-time, enabling organizations to detect and respond to cyber threats more effectively.

•   Behavioural Analysis: AI algorithms can identify patterns of malicious behaviour and anomalies, helping organizations detect sophisticated cyber-attacks that may go unnoticed by traditional security measures.

•   Automation: AI-driven automation can streamline security operations, reduce manual workload, and free up human resources to focus on strategic tasks and decision-making.

•   Predictive Analytics: AI can analyse historical data and predict future cyber threats, enabling organizations to proactively mitigate risks and prevent potential breaches before they occur.
Challenges:

• Data Privacy and Ethics: AI algorithms rely on vast amounts of data to train and improve their accuracy, raising concerns about data privacy, transparency, and potential biases in AI decision-making.

• Adversarial Attacks: AI models are susceptible to manipulation and exploitation by malicious actors who can launch adversarial attacks to deceive AI algorithms and evade detection.

• Lack of Explainability: AI-driven decisions may lack transparency and explainability, making it challenging for cybersecurity professionals to understand and trust AI-generated insights and recommendations.

• Overreliance on AI: Organizations must be cautious not to over-rely on AI-driven solutions and maintain human oversight to ensure the accuracy, reliability, and accountability of AI-generated outputs.

2. Internet of Things (IoT):

Opportunities:

- Improved Connectivity: IoT devices enable seamless connectivity and data exchange between physical objects, systems, and networks, enhancing operational efficiency and productivity.

- Real-Time Monitoring: IoT sensors can collect and transmit data in real-time, enabling organizations to monitor assets, infrastructure, and environments more effectively and respond promptly to emerging threats or anomalies.

- Predictive Maintenance: IoT devices can monitor equipment performance and predict maintenance needs, reducing downtime, minimizing costs, and enhancing operational resilience.

- Enhanced Decision-Making: IoT data analytics can provide valuable insights into consumer behaviour, market trends, and operational performance, empowering organizations to make informed decisions and drive innovation.

Challenges:

• Security Vulnerabilities: IoT devices often lack robust security features, making them vulnerable to cyber-attacks and exploitation by malicious actors to gain unauthorized access, steal sensitive data, or disrupt operations.

• Data Privacy Concerns: IoT devices collect vast amounts of personal and sensitive data, raising concerns about data privacy, confidentiality, and compliance with regulatory requirements such as GDPR.

• Interoperability Issues: IoT devices from different manufacturers may use proprietary protocols and standards, leading to interoperability issues and compatibility challenges that hinder integration and data sharing.

• Scalability and Complexity: Managing large-scale deployments of IoT devices can be complex and challenging, requiring organizations to implement robust governance, risk management, and compliance processes to ensure the security and integrity of IoT ecosystems.

3.   Blockchain:

Opportunities:

•   Immutable Ledger: Blockchain technology provides a decentralized and immutable ledger that ensures the integrity and transparency of transactions, making it suitable for applications such as secure data sharing, supply chain management, and digital identity verification.

•   Smart Contracts: Blockchain-based smart contracts enable automated and self-executing agreements, eliminating the need for intermediaries and reducing the risk of fraud, errors, and disputes.

•   Data Integrity: Blockchain can enhance data integrity and provenance by providing cryptographic verification and timestamping, enabling organizations to track the origin and lineage of data and ensure its authenticity and integrity.

- Decentralized Identity: Blockchain-based decentralized identity solutions offer individuals greater control over their personal information and authentication credentials, reducing reliance on centralized authorities and mitigating the risk of identity theft and fraud.

Challenges:

- Scalability: Blockchain scalability remains a significant challenge, with current blockchain networks facing limitations in transaction throughput, latency, and energy consumption, hindering their widespread adoption for large-scale applications.

- Regulatory Uncertainty: Regulatory frameworks for blockchain technology are still evolving, with legal and compliance challenges related to data privacy, security, and jurisdiction that may vary across jurisdictions and industries.

- Interoperability: Ensuring interoperability between different blockchain platforms and networks is essential for seamless data exchange and integration, but interoperability standards and protocols are still under development and may vary between blockchain ecosystems.

• Security Risks: While blockchain is inherently secure due to its cryptographic principles, vulnerabilities such as smart contract bugs, consensus algorithm flaws, and 51% attacks pose security risks that must be addressed to ensure the integrity and resilience of blockchain networks and applications.

In conclusion, the opportunities presented by artificial intelligence, Internet of Things, and blockchain in cybersecurity are vast and promising, offering organizations innovative solutions to enhance threat detection, improve operational efficiency, and ensure data integrity.

However, these technologies also bring new challenges and risks that must be addressed to realize their full potential securely and effectively. By understanding the opportunities and challenges of AI, IoT, and blockchain in cybersecurity and implementing appropriate strategies, organizations can harness the transformative power of these technologies to strengthen their cybersecurity defences, adapt to the evolving threat landscape, and achieve their cybersecurity objectives effectively.

Strategies for Anticipating and Mitigating Risks Associated with New Technologies

The rapid pace of technological innovation brings tremendous opportunities for organizations to enhance efficiency, productivity, and competitiveness. However, along with these opportunities come new risks and challenges that must be carefully managed to ensure the security, integrity, and resilience of critical systems and data. Anticipating and mitigating risks associated with new technologies is essential for organizations to harness the benefits of innovation while safeguarding against potential threats and vulnerabilities.

This book explores strategies for anticipating and mitigating risks associated with new technologies and outlines best practices for organizations to navigate the complex landscape of technological innovation securely and effectively.

1. Proactive Risk Assessment:

Conducting proactive risk assessments is essential for identifying potential risks and vulnerabilities associated with new technologies before they are deployed in production environments. Organizations should assess the potential impact of new technologies on their systems, networks, and data, as well as the likelihood of various risks occurring. This involves evaluating factors such as security vulnerabilities, data privacy concerns, regulatory compliance requirements, and business continuity risks. By conducting thorough risk assessments, organizations can anticipate potential risks and develop mitigation strategies to address them proactively.

2. Engagement with Stakeholders:
Engaging with stakeholders, including business leaders, IT professionals, cybersecurity experts, legal counsel, and regulatory authorities, is critical for identifying, assessing, and mitigating risks associated with new technologies. Organizations should establish cross-functional teams to collaborate on risk management initiatives and ensure that all relevant stakeholders are

involved in the decision-making process. By fostering open communication and collaboration among stakeholders, organizations can gain valuable insights into potential risks and develop effective risk mitigation strategies that align with business objectives and compliance requirements.

3. Continuous Monitoring and Surveillance: Implementing continuous monitoring and surveillance mechanisms is essential for detecting and mitigating risks associated with new technologies in real-time. Organizations should deploy monitoring tools and technologies that provide visibility into their systems, networks, and data, enabling them to identify anomalous activities, security breaches, and compliance violations promptly. By monitoring key performance indicators, security metrics, and compliance benchmarks, organizations can proactively detect and respond to emerging risks and threats before they escalate into significant incidents.

4. Adoption of Security Best Practices:

Adopting security best practices and standards is essential for mitigating risks associated with new technologies effectively. Organizations should follow established cybersecurity frameworks, such as NIST Cybersecurity Framework, ISO 27001, and CIS Controls, to ensure that they implement robust security controls and practices across their IT environments. This involves measures such as implementing strong access controls, encrypting sensitive data, conducting regular security assessments, and patching vulnerabilities promptly. By adhering to security best practices, organizations can reduce their exposure to cyber risks and enhance their overall cybersecurity posture.

5. Security by Design:

Incorporating security by design principles into the development and deployment of new technologies is essential for minimizing security risks and vulnerabilities from the outset. Organizations should integrate security considerations into the entire software development lifecycle, from requirements gathering and design to testing, deployment, and maintenance. This involves implementing secure coding practices, conducting security reviews and audits, and incorporating security testing and validation into the development process. By prioritizing security from the initial stages of development, organizations can build more resilient and secure technologies that are less susceptible to cyber threats and vulnerabilities.

6. Vendor and Supply Chain Risk Management:

Managing vendor and supply chain risks is crucial for mitigating risks associated with new technologies that rely on third-party components, services, or suppliers. Organizations should conduct due diligence on vendors and suppliers, assess their security practices and controls, and establish contractual agreements that address security requirements, responsibilities, and liabilities. Additionally, organizations should monitor the security posture of vendors and suppliers continuously and be prepared to take corrective action if security issues arise. By managing vendor and supply chain risks effectively, organizations can reduce their exposure to external threats and vulnerabilities associated with new technologies.

7.   Employee Training and Awareness:

Providing comprehensive training and awareness programs for employees is essential for mitigating risks associated with new technologies. Organizations should educate employees about the potential risks and security best practices associated with new technologies, such as phishing attacks, social engineering, and data breaches. This involves conducting regular security awareness training sessions, disseminating security policies and guidelines, and encouraging employees to report security incidents promptly. By empowering employees to recognize and respond to security threats effectively, organizations can strengthen their overall security posture and reduce the likelihood of security breaches.

8.   Regulatory Compliance and Governance:

Ensuring regulatory compliance and governance is essential for mitigating risks associated with new technologies, particularly in highly regulated industries such as healthcare, finance, and government. Organizations should stay abreast of relevant laws, regulations, and industry standards that govern the use of new technologies and implement policies and procedures to ensure compliance. This involves measures such as data protection, privacy controls, incident response planning, and regulatory reporting. By aligning with regulatory requirements and industry standards, organizations can mitigate legal and regulatory risks associated with new technologies and demonstrate their commitment to protecting sensitive information and maintaining trust with stakeholders.

In conclusion, anticipating and mitigating risks associated with new technologies is essential for organizations to navigate the complexities of technological innovation securely and effectively. By conducting proactive risk assessments, engaging with stakeholders, implementing continuous monitoring and surveillance, adopting security best practices, incorporating security by design principles, managing vendor and supply chain risks, providing employee training and awareness, ensuring regulatory compliance and governance, organizations can identify, assess, and mitigate risks associated with new technologies, minimize potential impacts on their operations, and achieve their strategic objectives in a rapidly evolving digital landscape.

Chapter 10: Case Studies and Lessons Learned

Case studies offer invaluable insights into real-world cybersecurity incidents, breaches, and vulnerabilities, providing organizations with valuable lessons learned and best practices for enhancing their cybersecurity defences.

By analysing past incidents and understanding the factors that contributed to their occurrence, organizations can identify potential risks, vulnerabilities, and gaps in their security posture and develop proactive strategies to mitigate future threats effectively. This chapter explores case studies from various industries and sectors, highlighting key lessons learned and actionable recommendations for improving cybersecurity resilience.

1. Equifax Data Breach:

The Equifax data breach, one of the largest data breaches in history, underscored the importance of timely vulnerability patching, secure configuration management, and robust incident response planning. Equifax failed to patch a known vulnerability in its Apache Struts software, which allowed cybercriminals to exploit the vulnerability and gain unauthorized access to sensitive consumer information. Lessons learned from the Equifax data breach include the importance of:

•   Prioritizing vulnerability management and patching critical vulnerabilities promptly.

•   Implementing secure configuration practices to minimize attack surfaces and reduce the risk of exploitation.

•   Developing and testing comprehensive incident response plans to detect, contain, and mitigate breaches effectively.

2.   WannaCry Ransomware Attack:

The WannaCry ransomware attack targeted organizations worldwide, encrypting data and demanding ransom payments in Bitcoin for decryption keys. The attack exploited a vulnerability in the Windows operating system, known as EternalBlue, which was leaked by the Shadow Brokers hacking group. Lessons learned from the WannaCry ransomware attack include the importance of:

•   Implementing robust cybersecurity hygiene practices, such as regular patching and software updates, to address known vulnerabilities promptly.

•   Deploying security solutions, such as endpoint protection, intrusion detection systems, and network segmentation, to detect and prevent ransomware attacks.

•   Educating employees about phishing threats and social engineering tactics to minimize the risk of malware infections and unauthorized access to systems and data.

3.   SolarWinds Supply Chain Attack:

The SolarWinds supply chain attack, attributed to the Russian state-sponsored hacking group Cozy Bear, targeted SolarWinds' Orion software platform, compromising thousands of organizations worldwide. The attackers inserted malicious code into SolarWinds' software updates, allowing them to infiltrate customer networks and exfiltrate sensitive information. Lessons learned from the SolarWinds supply chain attack include the importance of:

•   Conducting thorough supply chain risk assessments and due diligence on third-party vendors and suppliers to ensure their security practices and controls meet organizational standards.

•   Implementing security controls, such as code signing, digital certificates, and software integrity verification, to prevent tampering with software updates and mitigate supply chain attacks.

•   Enhancing threat detection and incident response capabilities to detect and respond to supply chain attacks promptly, minimizing the impact on affected organizations.

4.   NotPetya Cyberattack:

The NotPetya cyberattack, initially disguised as ransomware, spread rapidly across global networks, encrypting data and disrupting operations in various industries, including healthcare, finance, and manufacturing.

The attack leveraged the EternalBlue exploit, similar to WannaCry, to propagate within networks and cause widespread damage. Lessons learned from the NotPetya cyberattack include the importance of:

•   Implementing network segmentation and access controls to limit the spread of malware within organizational networks and mitigate the impact of cyber-attacks.

•   Backing up critical data regularly and storing backup copies offline to ensure data availability and integrity in the event of ransomware attacks or data breaches.

• Collaborating with industry peers, government agencies, and cybersecurity experts to share threat intelligence and coordinate response efforts during large-scale cyber-attacks.

5. Capital One Data Breach:

The Capital One data breach resulted from a misconfigured web application firewall (WAF), which allowed an attacker to exploit a server-side request forgery (SSRF) vulnerability and gain unauthorized access to sensitive customer data stored in the cloud. Lessons learned from the Capital One data breach include the importance of:

• Implementing secure coding practices and conducting regular security assessments and code reviews to identify and remediate vulnerabilities in web applications.

• Configuring cloud security controls, such as WAFs, access controls, and encryption, to protect data stored in cloud environments and prevent unauthorized access.

- Conducting comprehensive risk assessments and penetration tests to identify potential security weaknesses and gaps in cloud infrastructure and applications.

6. Lessons Learned and Recommendations:

- Prioritize cybersecurity hygiene: Regularly patch systems, update software, and implement security best practices to mitigate known vulnerabilities and reduce the attack surface.

- Implement robust security controls: Deploy endpoint protection, intrusion detection systems, firewalls, and access controls to detect and prevent cyber threats and unauthorized access to systems and data.

- Develop comprehensive incident response plans: Establish incident response teams, procedures, and protocols to detect, contain, and mitigate cybersecurity incidents effectively and minimize their impact on operations.

• Enhance supply chain security: Conduct supply chain risk assessments, monitor third-party vendors and suppliers, and implement security controls to mitigate supply chain risks and prevent supply chain attacks.

• Educate and train employees: Provide cybersecurity awareness training and education programs to employees, contractors, and stakeholders to raise awareness of cybersecurity risks and best practices and foster a culture of security throughout the organization.

In conclusion, case studies provide valuable insights into real-world cybersecurity incidents and breaches, offering organizations valuable lessons learned and actionable recommendations for improving cybersecurity resilience. By analysing past incidents, identifying common vulnerabilities and attack vectors, and implementing proactive strategies to mitigate risks effectively, organizations can enhance their cybersecurity defences, protect critical systems and data, and minimize the impact of cyber threats on their operations and stakeholders.

Examination of Cybersecurity Strategies
Implemented by Various African Governments

Cybersecurity has become a pressing concern for governments worldwide, including those in Africa, as they grapple with the challenges posed by rapidly evolving cyber threats and the increasing digitization of critical infrastructure and services. African governments are implementing various cybersecurity strategies to address these challenges and protect their citizens, businesses, and national interests from cyber-attacks, data breaches, and other malicious activities.

This book examines the cybersecurity strategies implemented by various African governments, highlighting their approaches, initiatives, and key achievements in enhancing cybersecurity resilience and mitigating cyber risks effectively.

1.   National Cybersecurity Policies and Strategies: Many African governments have developed national cybersecurity policies and strategies to provide a framework for addressing cyber threats and

vulnerabilities comprehensively. These policies outline the government's vision, objectives, and priorities for cybersecurity, as well as the roles and responsibilities of various stakeholders, including government agencies, private sector entities, civil society organizations, and international partners. For example, countries like Kenya, Nigeria, South Africa, and Ghana have established national cybersecurity strategies that focus on building cybersecurity capabilities, promoting cyber hygiene and awareness, enhancing law enforcement and regulatory frameworks, and fostering collaboration among stakeholders to strengthen cybersecurity resilience and combat cyber threats effectively.

2.   Capacity Building and Skills Development: Capacity building and skills development initiatives are essential for building a skilled cybersecurity workforce and enhancing cybersecurity capabilities at the national level. African governments are investing in training programs, workshops, and certifications to develop cybersecurity professionals with the knowledge and expertise needed to protect critical infrastructure, respond to cyber incidents, and mitigate cyber risks effectively.

For example, countries like Rwanda have established cybersecurity training centers and partnerships with educational institutions and industry stakeholders to provide cybersecurity training and certification programs for government officials, IT professionals, and law enforcement personnel, thereby enhancing the country's cybersecurity capabilities and resilience.

3. Cybersecurity Awareness and Education: Cybersecurity awareness and education campaigns are essential for raising awareness of cyber threats and promoting cyber hygiene practices among citizens, businesses, and other stakeholders.

African governments are launching public awareness campaigns, organizing workshops and seminars, and developing educational materials to educate the public about the importance of cybersecurity and the risks associated with cybercrime. For example, countries like Mauritius have implemented national cybersecurity awareness programs that target different segments of the population, including students, parents, teachers, and small and medium-sized enterprises (SMEs), to promote cyber hygiene, safe online practices, and cybersecurity best practices.

4. Public-Private Partnerships:

Public-private partnerships (PPPs) play a crucial role in enhancing cybersecurity resilience and fostering collaboration among government agencies, private sector entities, and civil society organizations. African governments are forging partnerships with the private sector, academia, and international organizations to share threat intelligence, exchange best practices, and coordinate response efforts to cyber threats and incidents. For example, countries like Senegal have established public-private partnerships with telecommunications companies, financial institutions, and cybersecurity firms to strengthen the country's cybersecurity capabilities, enhance information sharing, and promote collaboration in combating cyber threats.

5. Legislative and Regulatory Frameworks:

Legislative and regulatory frameworks are essential for establishing legal and regulatory requirements for cybersecurity and ensuring compliance with international standards and best practices. African governments are enacting cybersecurity laws, regulations, and policies to address emerging cyber threats, protect critical infrastructure, and enhance cybersecurity governance and accountability. For example, countries like Ghana have enacted cybersecurity laws and regulations that define legal frameworks for cybersecurity, establish responsibilities for government agencies and private sector entities, and provide mechanisms for cybercrime investigation, prosecution, and enforcement.

6.   Incident Response and Cyber Crisis Management:

Incident response and cyber crisis management capabilities are critical for effectively responding to cyber threats and mitigating the impact of cyber incidents on national security, public safety, and economic stability.

African governments are establishing national computer emergency response teams (CERTs) and cybersecurity incident response centers (CSIRTs) to coordinate response efforts, facilitate information sharing, and provide technical assistance and support to organizations affected by cyber incidents. For example, countries like South Africa have established national CERTs to respond to cyber threats, coordinate incident response activities, and provide guidance and support to government agencies, critical infrastructure operators, and other stakeholders in the event of cyber-attacks or data breaches.

In conclusion, African governments are implementing various cybersecurity strategies to address the growing threat landscape and protect their citizens, businesses, and national interests from cyber threats and vulnerabilities.

By developing national cybersecurity policies and strategies, investing in capacity building and skills development, raising cybersecurity awareness and education, fostering public-private partnerships, enacting legislative and regulatory frameworks, and enhancing incident response and cyber crisis management capabilities, African governments can strengthen their cybersecurity resilience and mitigate cyber risks effectively. However, challenges remain, including limited resources, skills shortages, and evolving cyber threats, which require continuous efforts and collaboration among stakeholders to address effectively and ensure a secure and resilient cyber environment for all.

Analysis of Successful and Failed Cyber Incident Responses

Effective cyber incident response is crucial for minimizing the impact of cyber-attacks, mitigating risks, and restoring normal operations promptly. Organizations around the world face an ever-evolving threat landscape, where cyber-attacks are becoming more sophisticated and frequent.

In this context, understanding the key factors that contribute to successful and failed cyber incident responses is essential for improving cybersecurity resilience and readiness. This book provides an analysis of successful and failed cyber incident responses, highlighting key lessons learned and best practices for organizations to enhance their incident response capabilities effectively.

1. Successful Cyber Incident Responses:
Successful cyber incident responses are characterized by timely detection, rapid containment, effective mitigation, and thorough recovery efforts. Key factors contributing to successful cyber incident responses include:

•   Preparedness and Planning: Organizations that invest in proactive incident response planning and preparation are better equipped to respond to cyber threats effectively. Successful incident response plans include predefined roles and responsibilities, clear escalation procedures, communication protocols, and response playbooks tailored to different types of cyber incidents. Regular training, tabletop exercises, and simulations help ensure that incident response teams are familiar with their roles and responsibilities and can respond effectively during a crisis.

•   Collaboration and Communication: Effective communication and collaboration among internal teams, external stakeholders, and partners are essential for coordinating response efforts and sharing critical information during a cyber incident. Successful organizations establish clear lines of communication, establish cross-functional incident response teams, and engage with relevant stakeholders, such as IT, security, legal, communications, and executive leadership, to ensure alignment and coordination throughout the incident response process.

• Real-time Threat Detection: Timely detection of cyber threats is critical for minimizing the impact of cyber incidents and preventing further damage to systems and data. Successful organizations deploy robust threat detection capabilities, such as intrusion detection systems (IDS), security information and event management (SIEM) systems, and endpoint detection and response (EDR) solutions, to monitor network traffic, detect suspicious activities, and identify indicators of compromise (IOCs) in real-time. Automated threat intelligence feeds and machine learning algorithms can help enhance threat detection capabilities and enable organizations to respond proactively to emerging threats.

• Effective Containment and Mitigation: Once a cyber incident is detected, organizations must act quickly to contain the threat and mitigate its impact on systems, networks, and data. Successful incident response teams leverage their knowledge of the organization's infrastructure and systems to isolate affected assets, block malicious activities, and prevent further spread of the attack. Implementing network segmentation, disabling compromised accounts, and deploying security patches and updates are common mitigation measures used to contain cyber incidents effectively.

• Thorough Recovery and Remediation: After containing the threat, organizations focus on restoring normal operations and remediating the effects of the cyber incident. Successful incident response teams prioritize recovery efforts based on criticality and impact, restore data from backups, and implement additional security controls to prevent similar incidents from occurring in the future. Post-incident reviews and lessons learned sessions help identify areas for improvement and inform future incident response planning and preparation efforts.

2.   Failed Cyber Incident Responses:

Failed cyber incident responses are characterized by delays in detection, ineffective containment, inadequate mitigation efforts, and incomplete recovery and remediation. Key factors contributing to failed cyber incident responses include:

•   Lack of Preparedness and Planning: Organizations that fail to invest in incident response planning and preparation are ill-equipped to respond effectively to cyber threats. Inadequate incident response plans, outdated playbooks, and insufficient training and resources can hinder response efforts and delay the containment and mitigation of cyber incidents. Without clear roles and responsibilities, communication protocols, and escalation procedures in place, incident response teams may struggle to coordinate response efforts and make timely decisions during a crisis.

•   Poor Communication and Collaboration: Ineffective communication and collaboration among internal teams, external stakeholders, and partners can hamper response efforts and exacerbate the impact of cyber incidents. Failure to establish clear lines of communication, engage with relevant stakeholders, and share critical information in a timely manner can result in confusion, misinformation, and misalignment during a cyber crisis. Without effective coordination and collaboration, incident response teams may struggle to prioritize response efforts, allocate resources, and make informed decisions to contain and mitigate the threat effectively.

• Inadequate Threat Detection: Organizations with limited threat detection capabilities are vulnerable to prolonged cyber-attacks that go undetected for extended periods. Inadequate monitoring, lack of visibility into network traffic, and reliance on outdated or ineffective security tools can impede the detection of cyber threats and increase the dwell time of attackers within the network. Without real-time threat detection and response capabilities, organizations may fail to identify cyber incidents until it is too late, allowing attackers to exfiltrate sensitive data, disrupt operations, and cause significant damage to systems and infrastructure.

• Poor Containment and Mitigation Strategies: Failure to contain and mitigate cyber threats promptly can result in the escalation of cyber incidents and exacerbate their impact on the organization. Ineffective containment measures, such as failure to isolate affected assets, block malicious activities, or implement security patches and updates, allow cyber attackers to maintain a foothold within the network and continue their malicious activities unchecked. Without a clear understanding of the organization's infrastructure and systems, incident response teams may struggle to implement effective containment and mitigation strategies, leading to prolonged downtime, data loss, and reputational damage.

• Incomplete Recovery and Remediation Efforts: Organizations that fail to prioritize recovery and remediation efforts risk prolonged disruptions to business operations and lingering vulnerabilities that could be exploited in future cyber attacks. Incomplete data restoration, inadequate security controls, and failure to address underlying security weaknesses leave organizations vulnerable to recurring cyber incidents and persistent threats. Without thorough recovery and remediation efforts, organizations may struggle to regain the trust of customers, partners,

Lessons Learned and Recommendations for Improvement in Cyber Incident Response

Effective cyber incident response is critical for organizations to minimize the impact of cyber-attacks, protect sensitive data, and maintain business continuity. However, navigating the complex landscape of cyber threats requires continuous learning, adaptation, and improvement. This book explores key lessons learned from past cyber incidents and provides recommendations for organizations to enhance their incident response capabilities and resilience effectively.

1. Lesson Learned: Proactive Preparation is Key Organizations must proactively prepare for cyber incidents by developing comprehensive incident response plans, conducting regular training and exercises, and establishing clear roles and responsibilities for incident response teams. Proactive preparation enables organizations to respond swiftly and

effectively to cyber threats, minimize downtime, and reduce the impact on operations.
Recommendation for Improvement:

• Develop and regularly update incident response plans to ensure they reflect the organization's current threat landscape, infrastructure, and systems.

• Conduct tabletop exercises and simulations to test incident response procedures, validate response plans, and identify areas for improvement.

• Provide regular training and awareness programs for employees, contractors, and stakeholders to ensure they understand their roles and responsibilities during a cyber incident.

2. Lesson Learned: Communication and Collaboration are Critical

Effective communication and collaboration among internal teams, external stakeholders, and partners are essential for coordinating response efforts, sharing critical information, and making informed decisions during a cyber incident. Clear communication channels, established protocols, and timely information sharing are key to a successful response.

Recommendation for Improvement:

• Establish clear lines of communication and escalation procedures for incident response teams, including contact information for key stakeholders and decision-makers.

• Foster collaboration among internal teams, external partners, and industry peers through information sharing, threat intelligence sharing, and joint response exercises.

• Implement communication tools and technologies to facilitate real-time communication and collaboration during a cyber incident, such as secure messaging platforms, conference calls, and incident response portals.

3. Lesson Learned: Timely Detection is Critical

Timely detection of cyber threats is essential for minimizing the impact of cyber incidents and preventing further damage to systems, networks, and data. Organizations must invest in robust threat detection capabilities, such as intrusion detection systems (IDS), security information and event management (SIEM) systems, and endpoint detection and response (EDR) solutions, to identify suspicious activities and indicators of compromise (IOCs) in real-time.

Recommendation for Improvement:

• Implement automated threat detection tools and technologies to monitor network traffic, detect anomalies, and identify potential security breaches in real-time.

• Leverage threat intelligence feeds, machine learning algorithms, and behavioural analytics to enhance threat detection capabilities and enable proactive response to emerging threats.

- Conduct regular security assessments and audits to evaluate the effectiveness of threat detection controls and identify areas for improvement.

4. Lesson Learned: Effective Containment and Mitigation are Essential

Organizations must act quickly to contain cyber threats and mitigate their impact on systems, networks, and data. Effective containment measures, such as isolating affected assets, blocking malicious activities, and implementing security patches and updates, are critical for preventing further spread of the attack and minimizing damage.

Recommendation for Improvement:

- Develop predefined playbooks and response procedures for containing different types of cyber incidents, such as malware infections, data breaches, and denial-of-service (DoS) attacks.

- Implement network segmentation, access controls, and endpoint security measures to isolate affected assets and prevent lateral movement of attackers within the network.

- Maintain up-to-date inventories of hardware, software, and network assets to facilitate rapid identification and containment of compromised systems.

5. Lesson Learned: Thorough Recovery and Remediation are Necessary

After containing the threat, organizations must focus on restoring normal operations and remediating the effects of the cyber incident. Thorough recovery and remediation efforts, including data restoration from backups, implementation of additional security controls, and post-incident analysis and review, are essential for minimizing downtime and restoring trust. Recommendation for Improvement:

- Develop detailed recovery and remediation plans that outline the steps and procedures for restoring systems, applications, and data from backups.

- Conduct post-incident analysis and review to identify root causes, lessons learned, and areas for improvement in incident response procedures and controls.

- Implement additional security measures, such as multi-factor authentication, encryption, and data loss prevention (DLP) solutions, to prevent similar incidents from occurring in the future.

6. Lesson Learned: Continuous Improvement is Essential

Cybersecurity is an ongoing process that requires continuous learning, adaptation, and improvement. Organizations must regularly assess their incident response capabilities, identify areas for improvement, and implement corrective actions to strengthen their cybersecurity posture and resilience effectively. Recommendation for Improvement:

- Establish a culture of continuous improvement by encouraging feedback, soliciting input from stakeholders, and prioritizing investments in cybersecurity resilience.

• Conduct regular reviews and audits of incident response procedures, controls, and technologies to ensure they remain effective and aligned with evolving threats and best practices.

• Engage with industry peers, cybersecurity experts, and regulatory authorities to stay abreast of emerging threats, trends, and regulatory requirements and incorporate lessons learned from past incidents into incident response planning and preparation efforts.

In conclusion, organizations must learn from past cyber incidents, adapt to evolving threats, and continuously improve their incident response capabilities to effectively mitigate cyber risks and protect their assets.

By proactively preparing for cyber incidents, fostering communication and collaboration, investing in threat detection capabilities, implementing effective containment and mitigation measures, conducting thorough recovery and remediation efforts, and embracing a culture of continuous improvement, organizations can enhance their cybersecurity resilience and readiness to respond to cyber threats effectively.

Chapter 11: Conclusion

The Path Forward: Strengthening Government Cyber Resilience in Africa

Cybersecurity has emerged as a critical concern for governments across Africa as they face a growing number of cyber threats and attacks targeting critical infrastructure, government agencies, businesses, and citizens.

The increasing digitization of government services, coupled with the rapid adoption of emerging technologies, has heightened the need for robust cybersecurity measures to protect against cyber risks and ensure the resilience of government systems and operations. In this book, we explore the path forward for strengthening government cyber resilience in Africa, highlighting key challenges, opportunities, and strategies for enhancing cybersecurity capabilities effectively.

1. Building Cybersecurity Awareness and Capacity:

Strengthening government cyber resilience in Africa begins with building cybersecurity awareness and capacity among government officials, IT professionals, and citizens. Governments should invest in cybersecurity education and training programs to raise awareness of cyber threats, promote best practices, and enhance cybersecurity skills and competencies.

This includes providing training on topics such as threat intelligence analysis, incident response, secure coding, and data protection. By empowering individuals with the knowledge and skills needed to identify and mitigate cyber risks, governments can enhance their overall cyber resilience and readiness to respond to cyber threats effectively.

2. Developing National Cybersecurity Strategies:

National cybersecurity strategies play a crucial role in guiding government efforts to strengthen cyber resilience and mitigate cyber risks effectively. African governments should develop comprehensive national cybersecurity strategies that outline their vision, objectives, and priorities for cybersecurity, as well as the roles and responsibilities of various stakeholders. These strategies should address key areas such as risk management, capacity building, incident response, regulatory compliance, and international cooperation. By developing clear and coherent cybersecurity strategies, governments can create a framework for enhancing cyber resilience and promoting a coordinated and strategic approach to cybersecurity across the public and private sectors.

3. Establishing Cybersecurity Governance and Coordination Mechanisms:

Effective cybersecurity governance and coordination mechanisms are essential for ensuring the coherence and effectiveness of government cybersecurity initiatives. African governments should establish dedicated cybersecurity agencies or departments responsible for coordinating cybersecurity efforts, developing policies and standards, and providing guidance and support to government agencies, critical infrastructure operators, and other stakeholders. These agencies should work closely with relevant ministries, regulatory bodies, law enforcement agencies, and industry partners to promote collaboration and information sharing and facilitate a unified response to cyber threats.

4. Enhancing Cyber Threat Intelligence and Information Sharing:

Timely and accurate cyber threat intelligence is critical for identifying and mitigating cyber threats effectively. African governments should invest in developing and enhancing cyber threat intelligence capabilities to monitor and analyse cyber threats, identify emerging trends and patterns, and anticipate potential cyber-attacks.

Governments should also promote information sharing and collaboration among government agencies, private sector entities, and international partners to facilitate the exchange of threat intelligence, best practices, and lessons learned. By fostering a culture of information sharing and collaboration, governments can improve their situational awareness and response capabilities and enhance their cyber resilience.

5. Strengthening Critical Infrastructure Protection:

Protecting critical infrastructure is paramount for ensuring the resilience of government systems and operations. African governments should prioritize the protection of critical infrastructure sectors, such as energy, transportation, healthcare, finance, and telecommunications, from cyber threats and attacks. This includes conducting risk assessments, implementing security controls and measures, and developing incident response plans tailored to the specific needs and vulnerabilities of each sector.

Governments should also work closely with critical infrastructure operators to enhance their cybersecurity capabilities, promote best practices, and address shared cyber risks and challenges.

6.   Promoting International Cooperation and Collaboration:

Cyber threats are inherently transnational in nature and require international cooperation and collaboration to address effectively. African governments should engage with regional and international partners, such as neighbouring countries, international organizations, and global cybersecurity forums, to share threat intelligence, coordinate response efforts, and promote best practices in cybersecurity. This includes participating in regional cybersecurity initiatives and forums, signing bilateral and multilateral agreements on cybersecurity cooperation, and contributing to global efforts to strengthen cybersecurity norms, principles, and standards. By fostering international cooperation and collaboration, African governments can enhance their cyber resilience and contribute to a safer and more secure cyberspace for all.

7.   Investing in Emerging Technologies and Innovation:

Emerging technologies such as artificial intelligence, blockchain, and the Internet of Things offer tremendous opportunities for improving government services and operations. However, they also introduce new cybersecurity challenges and risks that must be addressed.

African governments should invest in research and development initiatives to explore the potential applications of emerging technologies in enhancing cybersecurity resilience and mitigating cyber risks. This includes developing secure-by-design principles, implementing robust security controls and measures, and leveraging innovative technologies such as machine learning and automation to detect and respond to cyber threats more effectively. By embracing emerging technologies and innovation, African governments can strengthen their cyber resilience and stay ahead of evolving cyber threats.

In conclusion, strengthening government cyber resilience in Africa requires a comprehensive and multifaceted approach that addresses the key challenges and opportunities in cybersecurity. By building cybersecurity awareness and capacity, developing national cybersecurity strategies, establishing cybersecurity governance and coordination mechanisms, enhancing cyber threat intelligence and information sharing, protecting critical infrastructure, promoting international cooperation and collaboration, and investing in emerging technologies and innovation, African governments can enhance their cyber resilience and ensure the security, integrity, and resilience of government systems and operations in an increasingly digital and interconnected world.

Importance of Continued Investment in Cybersecurity Capacity Building and Infrastructure

Call to Action for Governments to Prioritize Cybersecurity as a National Priority

In today's interconnected and digitized world, cybersecurity has become a critical concern for governments worldwide. Cyber-attacks and threats are evolving rapidly, targeting governments, businesses, and individuals alike, with increasingly sophisticated techniques and tactics.

As the guardians of national security, economic stability, and public safety, governments must prioritize cybersecurity as a national priority to safeguard their citizens, critical infrastructure, and national interests effectively.

This book serves as a call to action for governments to recognize the importance of cybersecurity and take proactive measures to strengthen their cybersecurity posture and resilience.

1. Recognition of the Growing Cyber Threat Landscape:

Governments must acknowledge the growing cyber threat landscape and the increasing frequency and sophistication of cyber-attacks targeting government systems, critical infrastructure, and sensitive data. From ransomware attacks crippling essential services to nation-state-sponsored cyber espionage targeting government agencies, the breadth and depth of cyber threats facing governments are unprecedented. By recognizing the severity and urgency of the cyber threat landscape, governments can prioritize cybersecurity as a national priority and allocate the necessary resources, attention, and expertise to address cyber risks effectively.

2. Protection of National Security and Sovereignty:

Cyber-attacks pose significant risks to national security and sovereignty, threatening government institutions, military capabilities, and strategic assets. From cyber espionage campaigns targeting sensitive government information to cyber-attacks disrupting critical infrastructure and essential services, the consequences of cyber-attacks on national security can be severe and far-reaching. Governments must prioritize cybersecurity as a national priority to protect against cyber threats that undermine national sovereignty, compromise sensitive information, and threaten the integrity of democratic institutions and processes.

3. Preservation of Economic Stability and Prosperity:

The digital economy is the lifeblood of modern societies, driving economic growth, innovation, and prosperity. However, cyber-attacks targeting businesses, financial institutions, and critical infrastructure can disrupt economic activity, erode consumer trust, and undermine investor confidence. Governments must prioritize cybersecurity as a national priority to protect the digital economy from cyber threats that jeopardize economic stability and prosperity. By investing in cybersecurity measures and promoting a secure and resilient cyber environment, governments can foster trust, promote innovation, and ensure the continued growth and competitiveness of their economies.

4. Protection of Critical Infrastructure and Essential Services:

Critical infrastructure, such as energy, transportation, healthcare, finance, and telecommunications, underpins the functioning of modern societies and economies. Cyber-attacks targeting critical infrastructure can have devastating consequences, disrupting essential services, causing economic losses, and endangering public safety. Governments must prioritize cybersecurity as a national priority to protect critical infrastructure from cyber threats and ensure the resilience and reliability of essential services. By investing in cybersecurity measures, conducting risk assessments, and implementing robust security controls, governments can enhance the protection of critical infrastructure and safeguard the well-being and prosperity of their citizens.

5.   Defence against Cyber Espionage and Cyber Warfare:

Cyber espionage and cyber warfare pose significant threats to national security and geopolitical stability, with state-sponsored actors engaging in malicious cyber activities to steal sensitive information, disrupt government operations, and undermine strategic interests. Governments must prioritize cybersecurity as a national priority to defend against cyber espionage and cyber warfare and protect national sovereignty and interests. By strengthening cyber defences, enhancing threat detection capabilities, and fostering international cooperation, governments can deter malicious cyber activities and safeguard their national interests in cyberspace.

6.   Protection of Citizen Privacy and Civil Liberties:

As governments collect and store vast amounts of sensitive information about their citizens, protecting citizen privacy and civil liberties from cyber threats is paramount. Cyber-attacks targeting government databases, surveillance systems, and communication networks can compromise citizen privacy, infringe upon civil liberties, and erode trust in government institutions. Governments must prioritize cybersecurity as a national priority to protect citizen privacy and civil liberties and uphold democratic values and principles.

By implementing robust data protection measures, adopting privacy-enhancing technologies, and respecting legal and ethical norms, governments can safeguard citizen rights and freedoms in cyberspace.

7.   Promotion of International Cooperation and Collaboration:

Cyber threats are inherently transnational in nature and require international cooperation and collaboration to address effectively. Governments must prioritize cybersecurity as a national priority and engage with international partners, neighbouring countries, and global cybersecurity forums to share threat intelligence, coordinate response efforts, and promote best practices in cybersecurity. By fostering international cooperation and collaboration, governments can strengthen global cyber resilience, enhance collective defence against cyber threats, and promote a safer and more secure cyberspace for all.

In conclusion, governments must recognize cybersecurity as a national priority and take proactive measures to strengthen their cybersecurity posture and resilience effectively.

By prioritizing cybersecurity, governments can protect national security and sovereignty, preserve economic stability and prosperity, safeguard critical infrastructure and essential services, defend against cyber espionage and cyber warfare, protect citizen privacy and civil liberties, and promote international cooperation and collaboration. As the guardians of national interests and public safety, governments have a responsibility to ensure the security and resilience of their nations in cyberspace, and prioritizing cybersecurity is essential to meeting this responsibility effectively.

Appendix:

Glossary of Key Terms in Cybersecurity

1. Cybersecurity: Cybersecurity refers to the practice of protecting computer systems, networks, programs, and data from unauthorized access, cyber-attacks, theft, or damage.

2. Cyber Attack: A cyber-attack is a deliberate attempt by hackers or cybercriminals to compromise the confidentiality, integrity, or availability of computer systems, networks, or data.

3. Malware: Malware, short for malicious software, refers to software programs or code designed to infiltrate and damage computer systems, steal sensitive information, or disrupt operations. Common types of malwares include viruses, worms, trojans, ransomware, and spyware.

4.   Phishing: Phishing is a type of cyber-attack in which attackers use deceptive emails, messages, or websites to trick individuals into disclosing sensitive information, such as login credentials, financial data, or personal information.

5.   Social Engineering: Social engineering is a technique used by cyber attackers to manipulate individuals into divulging confidential information or performing actions that compromise security. Examples of social engineering tactics include pretexting, baiting, and pretexting.

6.   Denial-of-Service (DoS) Attack: A denial-of-service (DoS) attack is a cyber-attack that aims to disrupt or deny access to computer systems, networks, or services by overwhelming them with a high volume of traffic or requests, causing them to become unresponsive or unavailable.

7.   Data Breach: A data breach occurs when unauthorized individuals gain access to sensitive or confidential information stored on computer systems or

networks, potentially exposing it to theft, misuse, or disclosure.

8.   Encryption: Encryption is the process of converting plaintext data into ciphertext using cryptographic algorithms and keys to protect it from unauthorized access or interception during transmission or storage.

9.   Firewall: A firewall is a network security device or software program that monitors and controls incoming and outgoing network traffic based on predetermined security rules, policies, or access control lists (ACLs).

10.   Intrusion Detection System (IDS): An intrusion detection system (IDS) is a security tool or software program that monitors network traffic or system activity for suspicious or malicious behaviour and alerts administrators or security personnel to potential security incidents.

11.   Security Incident: A security incident is any adverse event or occurrence that poses a threat to the confidentiality, integrity, or availability of computer

systems, networks, or data, such as unauthorized access, data breaches, or malware infections.

12.   Vulnerability: A vulnerability is a weakness or flaw in a computer system, network, or application that could be exploited by attackers to compromise security, gain unauthorized access, or cause damage.

13.   Patch: A patch is a software update or fix released by vendors to address security vulnerabilities, bugs, or flaws in computer systems, applications, or firmware.

14.   Two-Factor Authentication (2FA): Two-factor authentication (2FA) is a security mechanism that requires users to provide two different forms of authentication, typically a password or PIN and a one-time code sent to their mobile device, to verify their identity and access a system or service.

15.   Cyber Resilience: Cyber resilience refers to the ability of organizations or systems to withstand, recover from, and adapt to cyber-attacks, disruptions, or incidents while maintaining essential functions and services.

16. Risk Management: Risk management is the process of identifying, assessing, and mitigating risks to an organization's information assets, systems, and operations, including cyber risks, to protect against potential threats and vulnerabilities.

17. Zero-Day Vulnerability: A zero-day vulnerability is a previously unknown or undisclosed software flaw or vulnerability that is exploited by attackers before a patch or fix is available from the vendor, leaving systems vulnerable to attack.

18. Incident Response: Incident response is the process of detecting, responding to, and mitigating security incidents, breaches, or cyber-attacks to minimize their impact on computer systems, networks, or data.

19. Digital Forensics: Digital forensics is the process of collecting, analysing, and preserving digital evidence from computer systems, networks, or storage devices to investigate security incidents, cyber-crimes, or unauthorized activities.

20. Cyber Threat Intelligence: Cyber threat intelligence is information collected, analysed, and disseminated about potential cyber threats, vulnerabilities, or adversaries to inform decision-making and enhance cybersecurity defences.

Further Reading

Additional Resources and References for Further Reading on Cybersecurity and African Government Departments

1. African Union Convention on Cyber Security and Personal Data Protection:

The African Union Convention on Cyber Security and Personal Data Protection provides a comprehensive framework for addressing cybersecurity and data protection issues in Africa. It outlines principles, obligations, and best practices for African governments to enhance cybersecurity resilience and protect personal data.

2. Africa Union Cybersecurity Strategy and Guidelines:

The Africa Union Cybersecurity Strategy and Guidelines offer guidance and recommendations for African governments to develop and implement national cybersecurity strategies, policies, and measures. It provides insights into regional cybersecurity challenges, priorities, and initiatives.

3. African Union Commission: Cybersecurity and Digital Transformation Division:

The African Union Commission's Cybersecurity and Digital Transformation Division provides resources, reports, and publications on cybersecurity-related topics, including policy guidance, capacity-building initiatives, and best practices for African governments and stakeholders.

4. Africa Cyber Security Culture Conference:

The Africa Cyber Security Culture Conference brings together cybersecurity professionals, policymakers, and experts from across Africa to discuss cybersecurity challenges, trends, and best practices. The conference provides valuable insights and networking opportunities for government departments and organizations involved in cybersecurity in Africa.

5. African Network Information Centre (AFRINIC):

AFRINIC is the regional Internet registry for Africa, responsible for allocating and managing IP addresses and AS numbers in the African region. AFRINIC offers training programs, resources, and publications on Internet governance, cybersecurity, and network security for governments, organizations, and technical professionals in Africa.

6. African Telecommunications Union (ATU):

The African Telecommunications Union promotes cooperation and collaboration among African countries in the field of telecommunications and ICT. The ATU provides resources, reports, and guidelines on cybersecurity, digital transformation, and ICT policy development for African governments and stakeholders.

7. Regional Economic Communities (RECs):

Regional Economic Communities such as ECOWAS, SADC, and COMESA play a crucial role in promoting regional integration and cooperation in Africa. Many

RECs have initiatives and programs related to cybersecurity, digital infrastructure, and ICT development, which can provide valuable insights and resources for African government departments.

8. International Telecommunication Union (ITU) Regional Office for Africa:

The ITU Regional Office for Africa supports African countries in the development and implementation of ICT policies, regulations, and projects. The ITU provides resources, guidelines, and capacity-building programs on cybersecurity, cybersecurity awareness, and ICT infrastructure development for African governments and stakeholders.

9. Cybersecurity Capacity Maturity Model for Nations (CMM):

The Cybersecurity Capacity Maturity Model for Nations (CMM) is a framework developed by the Global Cyber Security Capacity Centre (GCSCC) to assess and improve the cybersecurity capabilities of countries. African governments can use the CMM to evaluate their cybersecurity maturity and identify areas for improvement.

10.   Academic and Research Institutions:

Universities, research institutes, and think tanks in Africa conduct research and produce publications on cybersecurity, ICT policy, and digital transformation. Government departments can leverage academic and research resources for insights, analysis, and recommendations on cybersecurity-related topics.

Recommended Reading Books:

1. "Cybersecurity for Dummies" by Joseph Steinberg

• This beginner-friendly guide covers a wide range of cybersecurity topics, including threat detection, incident response, and risk management, making it suitable for government departments looking to build a foundational understanding of cybersecurity.

2. "Cybersecurity: A Practical Guide to the Law of Cyber Risk" by David A. Bodenheimer

• This book provides insights into the legal aspects of cybersecurity, including privacy regulations, data protection laws, and liability issues, which are essential considerations for Africa government departments managing cyber risks.

3. "Africa and Cybersecurity: Securing the Digital Frontier" edited by Houda Chakiri and Justin Williams

• This book offers perspectives on cybersecurity challenges and opportunities specific to Africa, including case studies, policy insights, and best practices for government departments seeking to enhance cyber resilience and mitigate cyber risks.

4. "The Cybersecurity Handbook: A Practical Guide to Profiting from Cybersecurity" by Dr. Marius Janson

• Dr. Janson's handbook provides practical advice and strategies for organizations to develop and implement effective cybersecurity programs, making it a valuable resource for Africa government departments seeking to manage cyber risks proactively.

5. "Cybersecurity for Everyone: Securing your home or small business network" by Marc Kranat

• This book offers practical tips and advice for individuals and small businesses on securing their networks and devices against cyber threats, making it a useful resource for Africa government departments supporting cybersecurity awareness and education initiatives.

6. "Managing Cyber Risk in the Financial Sector: Lessons from Asia, Europe, and the USA" edited by D. C. Wolf and W. Lemons

•   While focused on the financial sector, this book provides valuable insights into cyber risk management strategies, frameworks, and practices that can be adapted and applied by Africa government departments to safeguard critical infrastructure and sensitive data.

7. "The Cybersecurity Framework for Africa: Strategies for Policy-Making" by Sibusiso Sibisi and Alexander Clouter

•   This comprehensive guide offers practical strategies and recommendations for African policymakers and government departments to develop and implement cybersecurity frameworks, policies, and measures tailored to the unique challenges and opportunities in the region.

8. "Cybersecurity Essentials for Government Leaders: A Practical Guide" by Steve Caimi and William Corrington

• This book provides government leaders with essential insights into cybersecurity fundamentals, risk management principles, and governance strategies, making it a valuable resource for Africa government departments at all levels seeking to strengthen their cybersecurity posture.

9. "Cyber Resilience: The New Paradigm for Cyber Risk Management" by Mac Donley

• Mac Donley's book offers a comprehensive framework for building cyber resilience, including proactive measures, incident response strategies, and recovery planning, which are essential considerations for Africa government departments managing cyber risks effectively.

10. "African Cybersecurity Report 2022" by African Union Commission

• This report provides an overview of the cybersecurity landscape in Africa, including emerging threats, regional initiatives, and policy recommendations, serving as a valuable reference for Africa government departments seeking to stay informed and address cybersecurity challenges.

Q&A on Cyber-Security and Africa Government Departments

Questions:

1. What is the primary goal of cybersecurity?

a) To prevent all cyber attacks

b) To protect computer systems from unauthorized access, cyber-attacks, and data breaches

c) To ensure complete anonymity online

d) To monitor all internet traffic

2. Which African Union Convention addresses cybersecurity and personal data protection?

a) Abuja Treaty

b) Maputo Protocol

c) African Union Convention on Cyber Security and Personal Data Protection

d) Luanda Agreement

3. What is the purpose of the Africa Union Cybersecurity Strategy and Guidelines?

a) To promote cyber warfare
b) To provide guidance for African governments on cybersecurity
c) To discourage digital transformation
d) To limit internet access in Africa

4. What does the term "phishing" refer to in cybersecurity?

a) A method of catching fish online
b) Sending deceptive emails to trick individuals into disclosing sensitive information
c) Protecting sensitive information using encryption
d) Monitoring network traffic for suspicious activity

5. Which of the following is a common type of malware?

a) Firewall
b) Intrusion Detection System (IDS)
c) Ransomware

d) Two-Factor Authentication (2FA)

6. What is the purpose of a firewall in cybersecurity?

a) To block all internet traffic
b) To monitor and control network traffic based on security rules
c) To protect against physical intruders
d) To encrypt sensitive data

7. What does an Intrusion Detection System (IDS) do?

a) Detects and blocks suspicious network traffic
b) Encrypts sensitive data
c) Monitors physical access to buildings
d) Generates one-time codes for authentication

8. What is a data breach?

a) A secure communication channel
b) Unauthorized access to sensitive information
c) A type of encryption algorithm
d) A cybersecurity training program

9. What is encryption in cybersecurity?

a) Sending secure messages using encryption keys

b) Decoding encrypted messages

c) Hiding data from authorized users

d) Converting plaintext data into ciphertext

10. What is two-factor authentication (2FA)?

a) Using two different firewalls

b) Providing two different passwords

c) Verifying identity with two different authentication methods

d) Accessing two different networks simultaneously

11. Which organization is responsible for allocating IP addresses in Africa?

a) African Union Commission

b) International Telecommunication Union (ITU)

c) African Network Information Center (AFRINIC)

d) African Telecommunications Union (ATU)

12. What is the purpose of the Cybersecurity Capacity Maturity Model for Nations (CMM)?

a) To assess and improve the cybersecurity capabilities of countries
b) To create international cybersecurity regulations
c) To track cyber-attacks globally
d) To promote cyber warfare

13. What does the term "zero-day vulnerability" refer to?

a) A vulnerability that has been known for zero days
b) A software flaw that has been exploited before a patch is available
c) A type of encryption algorithm
d) A cyber-attack that occurs on the first day of the month

14. What is the purpose of digital forensics?

a) To encrypt digital data
b) To collect and analyse digital evidence
c) To hack into computer systems

d) To prevent cyber attacks

15.   What does "risk management" involve in cybersecurity?

a) Identifying and mitigating risks to information assets
b) Accepting all risks without mitigation
c) Encrypting all data
d) Ignoring cybersecurity risks

16.   Which of the following is NOT a common cybersecurity measure?

a) Installing antivirus software
b) Regularly updating software and systems
c) Sharing passwords with colleagues
d) Enforcing strong password policies

17.   What is the primary goal of cyber resilience?

a) To prevent all cyber attacks
b) To ensure complete anonymity online

c) To withstand, recover from, and adapt to cyber attacks

d) To monitor all internet traffic

18. Which organization promotes cooperation among African countries in telecommunications?

a) African Union Commission

b) International Telecommunication Union (ITU)

c) African Network Information Centre (AFRINIC)

d) African Telecommunications Union (ATU)

19. What is the primary purpose of the African Telecommunications Union (ATU)?

a) To promote cybersecurity awareness

b) To allocate IP addresses in Africa

c) To promote cooperation in telecommunications among African countries

d) To develop international cybersecurity regulations

20. What is the primary role of the International Telecommunication Union (ITU) Regional Office for Africa?

a) To develop cybersecurity strategies for African countries
b) To provide resources and guidance on cybersecurity
c) To promote cooperation in telecommunications and ICT development
d) To conduct digital forensics investigations

21. Which of the following is NOT a common cyber-attack?

a) Phishing
b) Ransomware
c) Antivirus
d) Denial-of-Service (DoS) attack

22.   What is the primary purpose of the African Union Commission's Cybersecurity and Digital Transformation Division?

a) To develop video games
b) To provide cybersecurity resources and publications
c) To promote cybersecurity awareness through social media
d) To organize cybersecurity conferences

23.   Which of the following is a common type of social engineering attack?

a) Firewall attack
b) Encryption attack
c) Phishing attack
d) Antivirus attack

Answers:

1. What is the primary goal of cybersecurity?
Answer: b) To protect computer systems from unauthorized access, cyber-attacks, and data breaches

2. Which African Union Convention addresses cybersecurity and personal data protection?
Answer: c) African Union Convention on Cyber Security and Personal Data Protection

3. What is the purpose of the Africa Union Cybersecurity Strategy and Guidelines?
Answer: b) To provide guidance for African governments on cybersecurity

4. What does the term "phishing" refer to in cybersecurity?
Answer: b) Sending deceptive emails to trick individuals into disclosing sensitive information

5. Which of the following is a common type of malware?
Answer: c) Ransomware

6.   What is the purpose of a firewall in cybersecurity?

Answer: b) To monitor and control network traffic based on security rules

7.   What does an Intrusion Detection System (IDS) do?

Answer: a) Detects and blocks suspicious network traffic

8.   What is a data breach?

Answer: b) Unauthorized access to sensitive information

9.   What is encryption in cybersecurity?

Answer: d) Converting plaintext data into ciphertext

10.   What is two-factor authentication (2FA)?

Answer: c) Verifying identity with two different authentication methods

11.   Which organization is responsible for allocating IP addresses in Africa?

Answer: c) African Network Information Centre (AFRINIC)

12. What is the purpose of the Cybersecurity Capacity Maturity Model for Nations (CMM)?

Answer: a) To assess and improve the cybersecurity capabilities of countries

13. What does the term "zero-day vulnerability" refer to?

Answer: b) A software flaw that has been exploited before a patch is available

14. What is the purpose of digital forensics?

Answer: b) To collect and analyze digital evidence

15. What does "risk management" involve in cybersecurity?

Answer: a) Identifying and mitigating risks to information assets

16. Which of the following is NOT a common cybersecurity measure?

Answer: c) Sharing passwords with colleagues

17. What is the primary goal of cyber resilience?
Answer: c) To withstand, recover from, and adapt to cyber attacks

18. Which organization promotes cooperation among African countries in telecommunications?
Answer: d) African Telecommunications Union (ATU)

19. What is the primary purpose of the African Telecommunications Union (ATU)?
Answer: c) To promote cooperation in telecommunications among African countries

20. What is the primary role of the International Telecommunication Union (ITU) Regional Office for Africa?
Answer: c) To promote cooperation in telecommunications and ICT development

21. Which of the following is NOT a common cyber-attack?
Answer: c) Antivirus

22. What is the primary purpose of the African Union Commission's Cybersecurity and Digital Transformation Division?

Answer: b) To provide cybersecurity resources and publications

23. Which of the following is a common type of social engineering attack?

Answer: c) Phishing attack

www.ingramcontent.com/pod-product-compliance
Lightning Source LLC
Chambersburg PA
CBHW071445220526
45472CB00003B/678